THE CONTEMPORARY CRUISE

Iwein Maassen

THE CONTEMPORARY CRUISE

Style • Discovery • Adventure

With 303 illustrations, 295 in color

Thames & Hudson

Text and photography by Iwein Maassen with the exception of the pictures on pages 12–15 and 21, Holland America Line; pages 16, 20, 74 top right, 78, 142–45 and 165, A. Dijkgraaf; page 34 top, C. Elfe; page 211, Deutsche Zentrale für Tourismus / Verkehrsamt Rüdesheim am Rhein; page 215, DZT / A. Cowin

Designed by Ronald van de Cappelle

Translated from the Dutch by Rebekah Wilson

© 2007 Iwein Maassen

First published in 2007 in hardcover in the United States of America by Thames & Hudson Inc., 500 Fifth Avenue, New York, New York 10110

thamesandhudsonusa.com

Library of Congress Catalog Card Number 2006908244

ISBN-13: 978-0-500-51349-1
ISBN-10: 0-500-51349-X

Printed and bound in Singapore by C.S. Graphics

Over 70% of the earth's surface is covered in water...

Contents

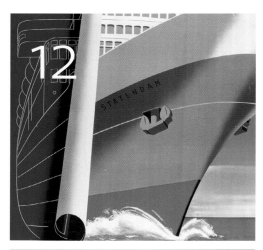

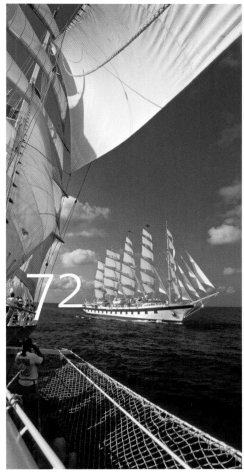

Cruising is a voyage of discovery where your hotel travels with you and you only have to unpack your suitcase once. Contrary to the common preconception, cruising is not just for older people: the average age of first-timers is now well below forty. The most important thing is to choose a cruise that suits you. For some people, the ship and all its facilities are a destination in themselves; for others, the ship matters less than the landscape or the ports of call. People with children will have different requirements from nature-lovers wanting to visit Antarctica. Some destinations can only be reached by water; in others, for example the islands of the Caribbean, a cruise enables you see so much more than a typical land-based vacation.

Sailing is a soothing experience. There are those who like to suggest it recreates the experience of the unborn child – back to the womb, so to speak. That may be overstating the case, but it's certainly true that sailing creates a welcome distance from the daily stresses and strains endured by most of us landlubbers. More and more people are discovering this, for the cruise industry is booming worldwide. Holidaymakers currently have the choice of more than 260 ships (large and small) on which to travel to around 2,000 destinations, and more ships are being built. And that is just sea cruises.

This book explores many different aspects of cruising, but it does not claim to be comprehensive. The intention is to open readers' eyes to the huge range of experiences that cruising encompasses. For there is much more to it than shown in the US television series *The Love Boat* – however fondly that show may now be recalled. But be warned: eighty-five per cent of people who choose this type of holiday seek to repeat the experience. Cruising is definitely addictive.

Iwein Maassen

Preface

I'm often asked, 'What's it like to spend the whole day sitting on a ship like that?' My answer is that being on a ship is wonderful and relaxing – but you don't spend the whole day on a ship! You sail in the evening and visit new destinations by day.

The history of cruising

If mankind had never had the opportunity to cross the oceans and make contact with other civilizations or trade with the inhabitants of far-flung continents, the world would be a very different place.

Back in the 17th century, the Dutch East India Company carried passengers on board its merchant ships, mostly to begin new lives on the other side of the world. But it was not until the 19th century that sailing for pleasure came into fashion, giving rise to cruising as we know it today.

The creation in 1837 of the Peninsular Steam Navigation Company, today's P&O, can be seen as the beginning of a new way of travelling. When, two years later, the Canadian Samuel Cunard acquired the sole rights to transport postal goods across the Atlantic and set up the British and North American Royal Mail Steam Packet Company (later renamed the Cunard Line), a new chapter in the history of cruising was opened. With the *Britannia* Cunard launched a regular transatlantic crossing that also carried passengers. When writers such as Charles Dickens and William Makepeace Thackeray wrote of their experiences on board, their readers' interest was aroused.

Passenger demand for such transatlantic crossings was boosted by large-scale emigration from Europe to the United States and Canada. But at the same time, the public (or, at least, the well-to-do) were becoming increasingly interested in sailing in style and in sailing as a vacation, and so ships had to be adapted to meet their requirements. The steamship *Ceylon* was thus renovated in 1881, and can be considered the first real cruise ship. The destinations it offered included the Canary Islands, the Mediterranean Sea, the Norwegian fjords and the Caribbean. As other ships followed, ever larger and faster, they gained a powerful hold over the public imagination. One of the most famous was the *Mauretania*, holder of the Blue Riband between 1907 and 1924. This unofficial trophy was awarded to the ship that made the fastest Atlantic Ocean crossing, and to win it was a triumph of national importance during this Golden Age of ocean liners. With a maximum speed of 25 knots, the *Mauretania* gained worldwide fame.

Travelling in luxury and style in an exclusive environment appealed

Left: **A Holland America Line advertisement from 1936.**
Above: **A 1953 poster promoting cruising.** Previous pages: **The sleek form of the cruise ship *Black Watch*, anchored at Belize.**

very much to the wealthier classes of Europe and the United States, and cruising became an increasingly popular pursuit at the beginning of the 20th century. Prohibition in the 1930s led to the invention of a new phenomenon, the so-called 'booze cruise'. What was forbidden to Americans on land was permissible at sea: drinking alcohol and gambling. As a result, short cruises became very popular, first solely because they enabled people to drink, but later also because of the destinations they visited. At the same time, these ships became larger, faster and more luxurious. The splendour of some of the finest ocean liners of the 1930s was without parallel, and cruising became synonymous with glamour. It was the ideal pastime for the rich and famous. American, British, German and French shipping companies began to compete to have the most prestigious ship. The French built the *Normandie*, which had aviaries of exotic birds in its winter garden. Cunard built two splendidly decorated ships, the *Queen Mary* and the *Queen Elizabeth*, which offered a weekly

service between Southampton and New York. Incidentally, the *Queen Mary* can still be enjoyed: it is now permanently docked at Long Beach, California, where it operates as a hotel.

With the outbreak of the Second World War came the abrupt end of an era. Governments requisitioned cruise ships, painted them grey and used them to transport military troops. After the war, the world was a different place. The only ship ever to hold the Blue Riband again was the *United States*. Cruise ships did resume service, but the aura of glamour that had surrounded them prior to the war was gone. They became once more a means of transport, a way of getting from one place to another. The destination was the purpose and not the journey itself.

With the arrival of mass air travel, the cruise companies found themselves facing a major competitor. In the 1960s, it was still cheaper to travel by ship; but that changed with the introduction of the Boeing 747 at the beginning of the 1970s. As air travel became ever more popular and affordable,

Holland-America Line

NIEUW AMSTERDAM

s good to be on a well-run ship"

many shipping companies went into bankruptcy. But others soldiered on, still convinced of the advantages of cruising. For there remained destinations that could only be reached by ship – including the Caribbean, which in those days was not served by any commercial flights. Cruise companies based themselves in Florida (for cruises to the Caribbean region), California (cruises to Mexico) and Vancouver (cruises to Alaska). The hugely popular television series *The Love Boat*, which began in 1977 and ran for nine seasons without a break on US television, did an enormous amount to spread the idea of a cruise as a vacation option. Ever more people began to realize that cruises were not just for the rich, they were accessible to everyone.

Left: **Cruising at the end of the 1950s.**
Opposite, top to bottom: **A poster from 1898;
An advert from NASM; Neptune on a 1950 poster
for the *Rijndam* and the *Maasdam*.**

Cruising today

Enjoying the whirlpool on the deck of the *Black Watch*. Opposite: Sunbeds await baskers on the *Westerdam*.

When in 1988 the Royal Caribbean's *Sovereign of the Seas* began her maiden voyage from Miami, she set the standard for cruising as we know it today. With the capacity to carry 2,276 passengers, she was the first true mega cruise ship, built for mass tourism at sea. This 'floating resort' gave a whole new meaning to the idea of the ship itself as the holiday destination, and provided the model for many ever more extravagant vessels that have been built since. These are not just big, they also offer a staggering variety of facilities and entertainments which may include swimming pools with chutes, whirlpools, spas, theatres, cinemas, shopping arcades, tennis courts, golf simulators, climbing walls, mini golf, bars, discotheques, restaurants and casinos. Such ships are like sailing holiday villages, with the captain as mayor.

The interiors of some of these new mega-ships are as extravagant as the hotels of Las Vegas. Some have as their prominent central feature a multi-storey atrium reminiscent of the interior of a modern cathedral, with neon-lit lifts flashing up and down. Other ship designers opt for a horizontal atrium, which often looks more like a modern covered shopping mall. None are more outrageously spectacular than the ships operated by Carnival Cruise Lines, designed by Joe Farcus in a style described as 'entertainment architecture'. This freely mixes and matches a multitude of inspirations. Imagine a bar decorated in ancient Egyptian style next door to a sleek sports bar with flat television screens showing non-stop video clips and sporting competitions. Other ships evoke the more restrained atmosphere of classic European hotels: chic with lots of dark wood, gleaming brass and authentic art throughout. The Holland America Line boasts about the lengths it went to acquire the ancient and modern art that adorns its ships.

The latest trend in the cruise world is staterooms with balconies. There is a huge demand for such lavish accommodation. And sure enough, anyone who has tasted the pleasure of calling such a stateroom home – albeit temporarily – would not want to cramp their style at sea with anything less ever again. But perhaps it is no surprise that in

Above and opposite: **The interior of the**
Grand Princess.

this age of the mega-ship, there is also an increasing demand for the absolute opposite: small, intimate ships. Because of their shallow draft, small vessels can sail to places inaccessible to such big ships. Tiny ports and bays hidden away from the outside world make charming ports of call, and are not subject to the sudden huge influx of people that a mega-ship brings. Such boutique ships aspire to give a maximum 200 or so guests the feeling of being on their own yacht. There is of course much less choice of entertainment than on a mega-ship, but this is precisely what appeals to their passengers. For many people they also create a sense of being closer to water and the elements. And of course the attraction of the intimate atmosphere, personal service and gastronomic pampering is not to be underestimated.

Between the mega and the boutique categories, there are two other main groupings: so-called small ships, which carry between 200 and 500 passengers; and medium-sized ships, which can accommodate between 500 and 1,500 passengers. And that is by no means all – there

are also cruises available on yachts, tall ships, expedition ships, freight ships and river boats.

In its essentials, cruising has changed little since its very earliest days. Now, as then, the on-board experience is all about relaxation and indulgence – about being utterly spoiled. Hence all modern ships have a good spa on board, and the newest ships often boast spacious health and beauty treatment facilities. As well as the latest fitness equipment (often positioned to give you a great view of the sea while working out), these ships also offer saunas and steam baths and a variety of relaxation treatments, ranging from body scrubs and hydrotherapy to shiatsu and hot stone massages.

The food on today's cruise ships is also often of high quality. Mega-ships lay on free food from morning till night, in addition to breakfast, lunch and dinner. We are talking 24-hour hamburger and pizza joints, after-midnight chocolate buffets, and room service throughout the day. In addition to the standard dining rooms, newer cruise ships increasingly offer a choice of small

speciality restaurants. These intimate alternatives have to be reserved and paid for separately, but are often extremely popular: many cruise lines bring in renowned chefs as consultants, and it is frequently necessary to make a reservation on the first day for a table on the last day of your cruise. With all that fine food on offer, it can be difficult to resist temptation, and gaining a few

The modern sushi bar on board the
Crystal Serenity.

pounds during the trip is a well-known phenomenon. But cruise companies have come up with a solution: menus often include tasty low-calorie choices and there is a range of on-board fitness activities to help keep extra pounds at bay.

Nowadays there are countless destinations to choose from. Old favourites such as the Caribbean and the European Mediterranean region continue to be popular, not just because of their warm climates and rich cultures, but also because of the stability of their political climates. Other parts of the world, such as the Baltic States and Russia, have become much more popular with cruisers and holidaymakers in recent years as their political circumstances have changed. There is also increasing demand for nature and expedition cruises. Alaska, with its magnificent glacier landscape, has long been popular. Princess Cruises and the Holland America Line operate their own hotels, coaches and even trains there. The pristine snowscape of Antarctica has been drawing increasing numbers of visitors in recent years. Cruise companies operating in such areas are subject to tight restrictions to ensure they do not threaten unique and delicate ecosystems.

Never before have there been so many cruises in different parts of the world. So whether you are a nature-lover, a fun-lover, an admirer of cultural sights, or simply wish to escape and relax in style, there is guaranteed to be a cruise to suit you.

Left: **Relaxing with a book on board the** *Westerdam.* Above: **On the Holland America Line, food is served on fine porcelain.**

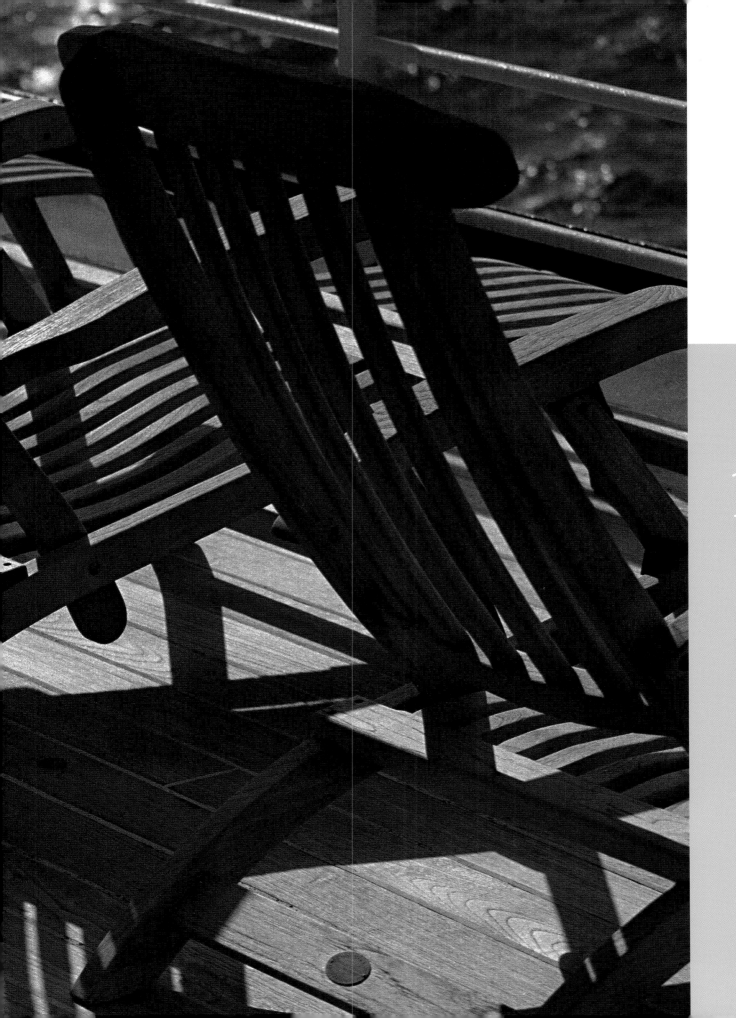

1

Legendary ships

As cruising continues to grow in popularity, so the choice of ships expands. Most modern ships fall into the mega-ship category – floating resorts that offer such a wide choice of entertainment that there can seem little need to disembark and explore the various ports of call. Different cruise companies often order identical vessels to keep costs down, thereby creating a sense of familiarity that does in fact appeal to many tourists. It's a competitive field, but the biggest cruise ship company in the world, Carnival, is also top of the pile when it comes to providing well-organized, fun-packed cruises on board ships whose fantastical decor defies all expectation. With high-energy nightlife, high-tech facilities, plenty of organized activities and lashings of razzle-dazzle entertainment, Carnival cruises are a winner, especially among a chiefly American, younger first-time cruise crowd.

At the opposite end of the scale is a new trend for boutique ships, such as stylish sister ships *Sea Dream I* and *Sea Dream II*, which offer a different kind of familiarity. These small craft aim to give passengers the intimate and exclusive feeling of being on their own yacht. One specially elegant classic is the *Sea Cloud* – a unique tall ship with a fascinating history that stretches back to the 1930s. Built as a private yacht, she retains her exclusive, luxurious feel despite lacking some of the features that regular cruisers might have come to expect. There isn't an on-board swimming pool, for example, but this doesn't mean you miss out: a selection of snorkelling, water-skiing and windsurfing equipment is available for use free of charge, and complimentary shore excursions take you to isolated, unspoiled beaches where you can swim and explore to your heart's content. The personal touch and exquisite surroundings on board the *Sea Cloud* make this a truly unforgettable cruising experience.

Opposite: **One of the rescue boats on board the *Queen Elizabeth 2*.**

Lifts streak up and down the atrium of the *Carnival Destiny*. Opposite: **Detail of the rigging on board the *Sea Cloud*.**

Sometimes it is the successful combination of classic and modern that gives a cruising experience the edge. Vessels built more than twenty-five years ago have usually been refurbished at some point, in some cases lavishly. The legendary *Queen Elizabeth 2*, for example, was built in the 1960s and refurbished in 1999 to the tune of $80 million. It may have low ceilings compared with its modern counterparts and a slightly awkward, disorientating layout – with the result that passengers are occasionally to be seen shuffling around corridors armed with floor plans – but what the *QE2* lacks in convenience it easily makes up for in personality. Robust and swift, it was built as an ocean liner for transatlantic crossings and even today retains its standing as one of the fastest passenger ships in the world.

Sea Cloud
Elegance
on the seas

The *Sea Cloud* is an authentic remnant of a bygone age with a wonderfully colourful history stretching across more than seven decades.

Originally called the *Hussar*, this four-masted barque was built in Germany in 1931 and bought by successful Wall Street broker E.F. Hutton. Hutton's wife, the hugely wealthy heiress Marjorie Merriweather Post, spent some two years working full time to create the interior of the vessel, the largest private yacht of its time, and the quality is second to none. She had a very thorough approach: staterooms were built to scale in a warehouse in Brooklyn in order to complete the design step by step before transporting everything to the ship. The antique furniture, paintings and other valuables for the staterooms were chosen with the utmost care, and many original features survive to this day.

The Huttons had a busy social life and frequently used the *Hussar* for both business and pleasure. After the breakdown of their marriage in 1935, Hutton gave the ship to his ex-wife because he knew how much it meant to her. Just four months after her divorce, Post married her childhood friend Joseph Davies, a lawyer and a diplomat. In 1937 Davies was sent to the USSR to head up the American embassy in Moscow. He took his wife with him and sent the ship, renamed the *Sea Cloud,* to St Petersburg (or Leningrad, as it was

The *Sea Cloud*'s former reception and dining room have now been merged to create a sumptuous restaurant and bar.

This page: **Details from Marjorie Merriweather Post's stateroom. The swan-shaped tap, below, is made of gold.**
Opposite above: **Ed Hutton's stateroom.**
Opposite below: **The corridor to the master bedrooms.**

called during the Soviet era). The *Sea Cloud* became a sort of 'floating palace', the ideal environment in which to receive important guests.

This extravagance was short-lived. With the looming threat of war, the ship was returned to the United States. After the Japanese attacked Pearl Harbor in 1941, the American navy commandeered many yachts for the war effort, but President Roosevelt – who, as a good friend of Davies, knew the *Sea Cloud* well – thought this one too handsome for military service. But her luck soon ran out: in 1942 the *Sea Cloud* had her masts removed, was painted grey, fitted with cannons, and chartered by the United States Navy for the token sum of $1 per year. Under the codename IX-99, she was sent off to serve as a weather station in the Azores and off the coast of Greenland.

The bridge still bears a plaque with five brass stripes: one for each half-year the *Sea Cloud* served the US Navy. Although the luxurious interior suffered a great deal, she was one of only a few private yachts to survive the war. In 1949, repainted white, she resumed her role as a hub of social activity, but by the beginning of the 1950s Marjorie Merriweather Post's marriage to Davies had hit crisis-point and she decided to sell the *Sea Cloud*. With the crew alone comprising seventy-two people, the maintenance was too much of a commitment. In 1955 the *Sea Cloud* was sold to the notorious dictator

The lower deck, which is mostly covered, is furnished with benches. The lunch buffet is served here in good weather.

of the Dominican Republic, Rafael Leónidas Trujillo Molina, who had visited the yacht on a number of occasions. He renamed her *Angelita*. When Trujillo's son Ramfis went to study in San Francisco, he used the yacht as his lodgings and became infamous for his on-board parties, at which stars such as Zsa Zsa Gabor and Kim Novak were regular guests. Rafael Trujillo was assassinated in 1961 and revolution broke out in the Dominican Republic; the new rulers, seeing no reason to keep the ship, renamed her *Patria* and put her up for sale.

The American John Blue, owner of Operation Sea Cruises, bought her a few years later, changed her name once again to *Antarna* and sent her to Naples for a complete restoration. On her return to the United States in 1968, Blue ran into a dispute with the American tax department, and the ship was held in Miami, where she remained for eighteen months until she caught the eye of teacher and adventurer Stephanie Gallagher. She had dreamed of setting up a floating 'Oceanic School' in which students could gain experience of other civilizations, languages and research alongside their regular studies, as well as

Zsa Zsa Gabor and Kim Novak were regular guests.

forming the crew. Gallagher signed a contract with Blue to hire the *Antarna*, but he then retracted the agreement and retained the ship's papers. Gallagher went ahead regardless, taking some ninety students with her; they even hoisted a pirate flag on the mast as a joke. Blue went in pursuit, waiting wherever the *Antarna* docked to take back his yacht. This he finally did in Panama, where she then remained for eight years without maintenance.

By the time the German captain Hartmut Paschburg spotted the yacht, she had fallen into a serious state of disrepair. He succeeded in persuading a number of German businessmen to form a consortium to buy her and, together with a team of around forty volunteers, they began repairing the *Sea Cloud* – once more under her old name – in order to make her seaworthy. The work was completed in October 1978 and the *Sea Cloud* set off for Hamburg, where she was greeted by a warm reception as she entered the port on 15 November. It had been a costly and lengthy exercise, but the historic ship had both been restored to her former glory and brought up to exacting modern standards.

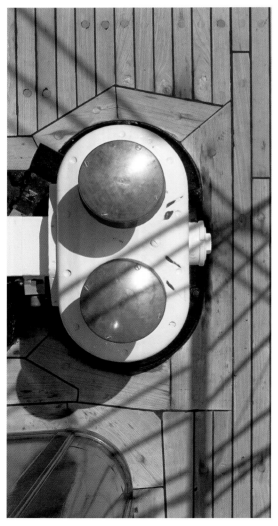

The *Sea Cloud* has thirty sails with a total surface area of 3,000 square metres (32,300 square feet). The main mast towers around 54 metres (177 feet) above the deck. Overleaf: The golden eagle, the *Sea Cloud's* figurehead.

Since 1979, when the *Sea Cloud* completed her first commercial cruise for her new owners, she has been universally admired. She cruises the Caribbean between December and March, and in April sets out towards the western and eastern Mediterranean, where she remains until the end of October. Though it is worth noting that the ship does not dock in US ports because the wood used in the interior and deck does not meet stringent American fire standards.

On board, the experience is of sumptuous luxury: the fully air-conditioned, 109-metre (358-foot) vessel has a sixty-man crew but accommodates just sixty-nine passengers in a total of thirty-four cabins. Most lavish are the two 'owners' suites' – exquisitely decorated with palatial fittings, they embody Post's taste with golden bath fixtures, marble, precious wood and antique furniture. Of course these opulent staterooms bear a princely price tag, but the ship has a further eight deluxe cabins, plus standard rooms. A panelled restaurant (the former salon) offers a range of continental nouvelle cuisine and local specialities, and there is an elegant bar on the promenade deck and a boutique. A cruise on board the *Sea Cloud* is a wonderful, once-in-a-lifetime experience – one you are guaranteed to want to repeat.

Carnival Las Vegas Cruising in style

From the outside, Carnival's ships may look fairly nondescript, but appearances can be deceptive: the company's fleet of twenty-two vessels offers the most extravagant cruises in the market.

The *Destiny* in the port of Antigua.
Opposite: **The enormous slide on board** the *Destiny*.

Entering the atrium of the *Fascination* can be slightly disorientating: it's more like a cathedral than a ship, albeit a very modern and thoroughly secular one. It's lined with shops selling everything from clothing to luxuries such as perfume and jewelry. Neon-trimmed lifts streak up and down the seven-storey space. Each level is impressively lit, and an enormous work of art dominates the central area. The theme running through the ship is 'Hollywood'. A collection of life-size dummies of famous film stars populates the public spaces. You may find yourself standing next to a stock-still Elvis when you order a drink. Further on Humphrey Bogart sits motionless at the bar, his glass untouched. A 'map of the stars' is available from the information centre showing the location of each figure and, given the size of the ship – which can accommodate over 2,000 passengers – it's a handy service if you want to make the most of the photo opportunities alongside silver-screen legends.

The glitzy Point After Dance Club on the *Destiny*. Far right: Staff in bright clothes serve cocktails in equally colourful plastic glasses.

The keyword here is fun. For many years American architect Joe Farcus has been responsible for the interiors of Carnival's cruise ships, which are designed to transport you temporarily into another world. He is also renowned for the signature winged 'whale tail' smokestack – nicknamed the 'Farcus Funnel' within the company – which decorates the fleet. Farcus calls his style 'entertainment architecture', and it is based on the principle that passengers should be bowled over each and every time they enter a room. You might not choose to let him loose on your house, but there is no doubting his ability to create a truly jaw-dropping experience. There is always a central theme running through each ship's design, whether that is for example the arts (*Inspiration*), cities of the world (*Carnival Triumph*), ships of the past (*Paradise*) or fabulous fictional icons (*Carnival Miracle*), and in each case particular attention is lavished upon the atrium, always the most impressive feature. Occasionally whimsical, often dramatic, always

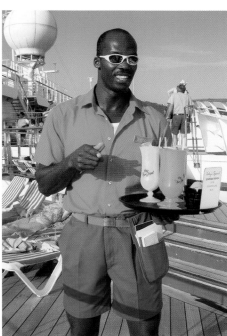

spectacular, Farcus's fearless mixing and matching of colours, themes and inspirations makes a tour of these extraordinary vessels a dazzling experience.

Initially, this flamboyant style attracted mainly young Americans, but nowadays there are also a large number of grandparents wanting to take their grandchildren on holiday with them. But given the high-energy, upbeat ambience, it's no surprise that the passenger profile remains relatively young – around 75 per cent of all passengers are under fifty-five, and 30 per cent are under thirty-five. The company particularly welcomes newlyweds, and it is even possible to get married on some ships, which have a special 'wedding chapel'.

Founded in 1972 by the late cruise industry pioneer Ted Arison, the Carnival Corporation has been hugely successful, over the years acquiring Princess

Left to right: **Bright stools in the swimming pool; The atrium on the** *Fascination*; **The casino on the** *Destiny*; **A detail of the swimming pool.**

Cruises, the Holland America Line, Cunard, Windstar Cruises, Costa Cruises and the Yachts of Seabourn. Today Carnival is the largest shipping company in the world, and the United States is still its biggest market and the departure point for nearly all of its cruises. It operates voyages to the Bahamas, the Caribbean, Mexico, Hawaii, Alaska, New England, Canada, Bermuda, Europe and the Greek Isles.

Carnival's cruise ships are a destination in themselves and are designed so that holidaymakers need never disembark. Food is available quite literally all day long, whether you want pizza at 10 a.m., around-the-clock room service, or a night-time snack at one of the lavish midnight and chocolate buffets. Every day there are numerous organized events and entertainments, from 'Mister Hairy Chest' competitions around the pool, Austin Powers dance classes, art auctions and bingo, to glitzy music and dance spectaculars in the evenings. Comedians, bands and musicians perform

nightly. On the decks, background music is played through loudspeakers during the day, while waiters and waitresses in vibrantly coloured clothing serve cocktails in equally garish plastic glasses. Babysitting is available, and an extensive programme of activities and entertainments will keep children of all ages happily occupied. At night the amusement machine is cranked up to full capacity: in one bar there is a jazz band, in another karaoke, while the disco reverberates to the latest hits until the early hours. The casinos, which are open during the day on the open sea, are also very popular.

If you do fancy exploring the various ports of call, there is a wide choice of excursions available. On a Caribbean cruise to tax-free St Thomas in the US Virgin Islands, for instance, one of the busiest ports of call in the world, you can choose between dozens of shore activities. Of course shopping rates high on many people's list, but other options range from visits to

Above: **Enjoying a cocktail on deck.**
Right and opposite: **The sun deck on the**
Fascination; **Steps on the outside deck**
of the *Destiny*.

the idyllic Magen's Bay to a spectacular seabed sightseeing trip in one of
Carnival's underwater scooters – no diving experience required.

All your needs will be catered for on a Carnival cruise, and you are free to do
as much or as little as you like. Of course this would not be the right choice
for anyone wanting to read a book on deck in peace or to enjoy the simple
tranquillity of sailing from one destination to the next. It can be a struggle
to escape the throngs of people and noise. But for high-energy, sociable
fun and entertainment, Carnival is number one.

Queen Elizabeth 2

The Grande Dame

Queen Elizabeth 2

of the cruiseworld

For years the *Queen Elizabeth 2* was the only ship offering regular transatlantic passenger crossings. Since the launch of the *Queen Mary 2* in 2004, which has taken over this task, she now ventures further afield, undertaking an annual world cruise as well as a range of shorter trips.

The imposing bow of the *QE2*.
Opposite: **The smokestack in the familiar Cunard colours.**

The *QE2*, as she is known for short, has an impressive service record. The shipping company Cunard announced its plans to build a new liner in 1959, but it was another ten years before the *QE2* set out on her maiden voyage. At the end of her first transatlantic crossing from Southampton to New York in 1969, she received a very enthusiastic welcome.

That voyage marked the beginning of a tradition that was to last decades. It was intended from the outset that the *QE2* would not just serve as a liner but also as a cruise ship. As a liner she had to have enough space to transport cars and large amounts of furniture; as a cruise ship she needed all the requisite facilities for hosting and entertaining passengers. In meeting that need, no corners were cut. Even the luxury British department store Harrods opened a branch on the ship. Cunard commissioned the cream of British designers, under the leadership of James Gardner, to create the *QE2*'s modern interior, which embodied all the high style of the Swinging Sixties.

Object of some controversy was the ship's funnel. In order to keep it in line with the style of the rest of the ship, the designers chose to paint it white. That was something of a shock to many people, for it marked a break with years of tradition: until then, the funnels on all Cunard ships had been red and black, making them instantly recognizable. But white it remained until 1982, when the British government called on the *QE2* to transport troops in the Falklands war. Once this service was completed the ship was repainted, with a red and black funnel.

The *QE2* combines grace and style with considerable power. She is still the fastest cruise ship in the world, with the largest cruise ship engine

A few small improvised bars have been set up. The champagne is flowing freely.

Comfortable seats enhance the journey.
Opposite: **Deckchairs await the first guests.** Overleaf: **The lobby on Deck 2.**

in the world. She can reverse faster than many modern cruise ships go forwards, and has a top speed of 32.5 knots. In 1970 she was able to make a transatlantic crossing in three days, twenty hours and forty-two minutes; at that time, her average speed was 30.36 knots. The QE2 was given such powerful engines because she was designed for transatlantic crossings, and weather on the Atlantic Ocean can be extremely turbulent. Over the years, she has been renovated numerous times and adapted to

meet modern requirements. The last time this happened was in 1999 when Carnival Corporation, the new owner of Cunard, gave her a facelift. Indeed, by 1996 Cunard had invested more than ten times the original construction costs in multiple renovations, including modification of the engines.

The Cunard terminal on the Eastern Docks of the Southampton pick-up point is full of hustle and bustle when I arrive to board the QE2 for a spell in the Mediterranean sun. Cars, taxis and immense limousines are coming and going. Porters stand ready to take passengers' luggage and ensure it is delivered to the correct cabin or suite. An agreeable feeling of luxury quickly takes hold of me. Relieved of my two heavy suitcases, I stroll over to the check-in desk and have a photo taken for my ship pass, a type of credit card that can be used to pay for everything once on board. Cabin 2076, Deck 2: my suitcases

50 Legendary ships

A bedroom in one of the QE2's suites.
Opposite: **Light filters through a porthole.**

safety drill, the loud ship's horn announces that is time to depart. Music can be heard on the outside decks and a few small improvised bars have been set up. The champagne is flowing freely.

are already waiting for me when I arrive at my ultra-comfortable and spacious cabin, with its immense double bed, separate seating area, television, air-conditioning, refrigerator and full bathroom with tub and shower. Just as I am about to open my complimentary bottle of champagne, the cabin stewardess arrives to enquire – in impeccable English – whether everything is to my satisfaction. 'No problem, Sir' is her response to my request to have my suit dry-cleaned in time for the evening. After the obligatory

Seats in the *QE2*'s restaurants are allocated according to room number. Apart from the Lido, this means that you can't just go into any restaurant to dine. It's an old-fashioned tradition, carried over from the time when ship passengers were separated into entirely separate classes, and it may not be to everyone's liking, so it's something to bear in mind when you book. I was lucky enough to have a seat in the Queen's Grill, the *QE2*'s finest restaurant according to those in the know. After just one meal, I was in complete agreement. The 'Rendezvous of Shrimps, Scallops and Oysters in Puff Pastry Bouchée with Leaf Spinach, Turned Vegetables and Chablis White Wine Dill Sauce' was truly first-class, as

You can't fail to arrive fully relaxed.
Right: **The *Queen Elizabeth 2* on the quayside in New York, where she is a regular visitor.**

was the service. Food is included in the price of the cruise, but drinks – aside from water, coffee and tea – are not. The lavish wine list has around two hundred different wines from eleven countries. The 'Connoisseur Wine List' features top wines such as Château Petrus, and prices that climb above $500. That will come as no surprise to connoisseurs, but the number of champagnes on offer might: famous brands such as Dom Perignon and Louis Roederer Cristal are just two choices from a no fewer than thirty-

seven. With an average of two hundred bottles consumed each day, champagne has long been a popular drink on board the *QE2*.

Since the Queen Mary 2 entered service, the *QE2* has operated as a full-time cruise ship rather than a liner, but it is no ordinary cruise ship. Designed to be able to navigate the Panama Canal, the *QE2* is perfectly suited to sailing to the most diverse destinations. She completed her first world cruise in 1975, and continues to undertake

regular world cruises to this day.
This classic ship has hosted many
a special guest: heads of state such
as Britain's Queen Elizabeth, the
Sultan of Brunei and the Emperor of
Japan; musical legends Mick Jagger,
Count Basie and David Bowie; and
film stars such as Elizabeth Taylor,
John Travolta and Meryl Streep.
For sumptuous style, rich history
and sheer glamour, there can be
few experiences to beat a cruise on
board the *QE2*.

2

Alternative cruises

Within the broad category of cruising there is huge amount of choice. Whether you are new to the experience or have already been on a number of cruises and are looking for something different, there is plenty of opportunity to find alternatives to suit you.

For those who like to keep the land in sight, one option is to take a barge trip or river cruise (see page 192). If you like to sail on the sea but still don't want to go too far from the land you could opt for a coastal cruise, whose ships sail no further than 32 kilometres (20 miles) away from the shore. The atmosphere on board is usually particularly informal, although there can of course be exceptions, but what is true of all these ships is that there is not much evening entertainment – passengers are left to amuse themselves, though during the day they are able to make excursions that can be booked on the ship.

Even organized excursions are not available on a freight ship, where passengers are left even more to their own devices, both during the day and in the evening. So if you are the type of person who would like to meet as many people as possible on your cruise and cannot get enough of cocktails and casinos, discos and organized entertainment, such a cruise is obviously not for you. However, freight ship cruises are available all over the world and offer an experience that feels like a genuine adventure, especially in the case of a cruise on board a tramp ship, whose precise course and ports of call will be determined only as the journey proceeds. A freight ship cruise will give you a glimpse into the life of today's professional sailors and busy industrial ports – a fascinating world that few outsiders ever get to see. It can also be a welcome way of bringing a cruising holiday within the reach of a more modest budget.

Opposite: **The stern of the Hurtigruten** *Kong Harold,* **which sails up the coast of Norway from Bergen to deep into the Arctic Circle.**

A cruise on a tall ship remains a very special experience. Watching the billowing sails, listening to the sea slap against the hull and the tautly pulled ropes chafe, feeling the wind in your hair – it never ceases to be romantic. Tall ships are much smaller than the average cruise ship, and that gives one the sense of being closer not just to the water but to nature itself. You feel the elements more intensely, especially the wind, that basic requirement for a sailing ship. Moving through the water with a swan-like grace, tall ships evoke all the emotion and romance of the legendary era of sailing ships. It is also eternally interesting to watch sailors at work, especially when you are lazing in a deckchair with a cool drink. The multitude of tasks involved in sailing such a ship is fascinating. And of course there is the ongoing maintenance: sailors repairing sails on the deck with a treadle sewing machine, or suspended high above the water painting a yard. It could only happen on a tall ship.

Flat-bottomed boats in the Dutch port of Hoorn at daybreak. Opposite: **A sailor carries out maintenance on a tall ship.**

From postal ship to cruise ferry

Hurtigruten

Every day, 365 days of the year, a Hurtigruten ship leaves Bergen in Norway to travel to the town of Kirkenes on the Russian border, far above the Arctic Circle.

It takes six days to reach Kirkenes after which the ship turns around and sets off back to Bergen again. The twelve-day trip covers some 2,500 sea miles (4,630 kilometres) and passes the unforgettably beautiful Norwegian coastline of fjords, islands and mountains, dotted with dozens of fascinating towns and villages.

The flag at the rear of the *Kong Harold* recalls the original function of the Hurtigruten. Opposite: **The resplendent colours of a Norwegian sunset.**

Hurtigruten literally means 'express service'. It began as a postal and goods service to settlements on the western Norwegian coast that historically were difficult to reach by land. Goods transportation still accounts for 25 per cent of turnover, but tourists have become increasingly important for the company. The ships make around thirty stops each way according to a set timetable. In larger places such as Trondheim, they dock for six hours. In smaller destinations, the ships stay for no longer than fifteen minutes; and in tiny ones the stop is five minutes maximum, just long enough for passengers to embark or disembark.

When, in 1891, the shipping advisor to the Norwegian government, August Kriegsman Gran, first proposed launching a rapid sea service between Trondheim and Hammerfest, the suggestion was dismissed out of hand by most shipping companies. It was thought much too dangerous: sailing during the winter, in conditions of round-the-clock darkness and harsh winds, was considered impossible. But one relatively young shipping company, Vesteraalens Dampskibsselskab, felt up to the challenge. Captain Richard With and his pilots spent a good deal of time mapping out the precise route, taking careful account of sea currents. They believed it was perfectly possible to establish a year-round express service, with a compass and clock sufficing as navigation tools, even in the dark and inclement winter. In May 1893, the young firm signed a four-year contract with the government, in which the latter agreed to support the organization of a weekly scheduled service between Trondheim and Hammerfest in the summer and between Trondheim and Tromsø in the winter. Some nine ports would be called at en route.

Captain With's plans had the benefit of one significant oceanic phenomenon: despite their northern latitude, Norwegian ports remain free of ice in winter thanks to the North Atlantic Gulf Stream, a current that has its

Huskies wait impatiently, anxious to get on with the job.
Left: **The splendid cloud clusters of the far north.** Previous
pages: **Panoramic views from the** *Kong Harold*.

source in the Caribbean. There, the water is warmed
to sub-tropical temperatures, before passing alongside
Mexico and the coast of North America, then across
the Atlantic and past the north coasts of Scotland
and Iceland. Finally it reaches Norway. By this time
it has of course cooled down considerably, but the
water still has a temperature of above 5° Celsius (41°
Fahrenheit), meaning that the Norwegian ports remain
accessible all through the year.

The departure of the steamboat *Vesteraalen* from
Trondheim on the morning of 2 July 1893 launched
a new era for the coastal populations of western
Norway. Until then, a letter originating in Trondheim
would take up to three weeks in summer and as
long as five months in winter to reach a recipient

in Hammerfest. From now on it took just a few days. Indeed the first post ship dropped anchor at Hammerfest on 5 July at 3.30 a.m., a full half hour ahead of schedule. All along the coast the ship and its crew were greeted with cheering and salutes.

Now that the feasibility of the route had been proven, more shipping companies came forward and the route was gradually extended. In 1898, Bergen was incorporated as the southernmost port; and in 1914, Kirkenes became the end destination. A Hurtigruten ship has set off from Bergen every day since 1936 – the service has only ever been interrupted during wartime. The fleet is now made up of eleven ships, though these have changed a great deal over the years. Goods and post are still transported, and local residents also make regular use of this express ferry service. Local passenger numbers declined after the Second World War, as the road network expanded and air transport increased. But that shortfall was offset by a new sort of passenger: the tourist. In recent years, the ships have been increasingly adapted to their requirements, so that nowadays the newest ships have facilities to match those of most cruise ships, with saunas, swimming pools, whirlpools, sundecks, viewing lounges and Internet access, not to mention around three hundred cabins and a number of suites. It is also possible to book organized excursions at some ports of call. If there is snow, one of the most popular activities is a trip on a husky sledge. On board, the ships also cater to passengers who are only making a brief trip, with facilities such as 'quick bite' cafeterias that are open

A striking lighthouse near Lofoten Opposite and overleaf: **The constantly changing views from the ship are impressive.**

twenty-four hours a day. Cars can also be taken on board, although camper vans are excluded.

The combination of tourists making the whole journey and local residents taking a short trip gives the on-board atmosphere a unique quality. As you sail along the coast the rugged landscape changes each moment, becoming ever more impressive. High in the north, the sun often creates enchanting lightshows, turning the sky now red, now purple, now orange. For a period in summer the sun never sets. As winter deepens the light takes on a pale delicate quality, and eventually disappears altogether. The magical Northern Lights regularly illuminate the night sky between the beginning of September and mid-April. This is not merely a cruise, it is a voyage of discovery of the sublime beauty of the Norwegian landscape.

Tall ships Sails, ropes, romance

Anyone who wants to experience the romance of the sea as it was in times gone by, who loves wind, freedom and sails (but also luxury), should consider a cruise on the finest of all sailing ships: a tall ship

Opposite: **The imposing masts and complex rigging of the *Royal Clipper* in the evening sun.**

ou would think they would be used to boats on Martinique. The high-tech toys of the rich and famous are everywhere, glittering in the sun. However, it is an antique-looking tall ship that steals the show here, as everywhere: no sooner does the *Star Clipper* begin to hoist her sails, than people get out of their seats, video cameras are quickly retrieved from bags, and tourists look on breathless. The sails take wind, swell, and without a sound the *Star Clipper* glides off, graciously turning her back on the coast.

Admiring the *Star Clipper* from afar is a thrill, but it doesn't come close to the experience of being on board. Leaning nonchalantly over the railing, owner Mikael Krafft considers his audience with amusement. 'Of course, it is a terrific show for everyone. They are looking at the past. A tall ship with full sails like this four-master gives off a unique sense of nostalgia and romance. Surely she is much more impressive than a modern luxury motor yacht?'

She might exude all the romance of the past, but this ship also has plenty of up-to-date luxury of her own. She may look old, but she is actually extremely modern – built in 1992 – and boasts every comfort. Two swimming pools, cabins with air-conditioning, telephone and television: these are just a few of the things that make the stay on board pleasurable.

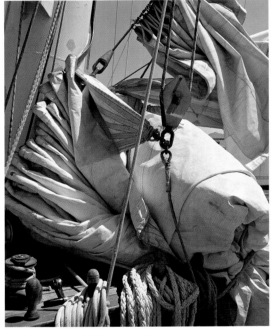

White sails and blue skies complete the
romantic picture on board the *Star Clipper*.
Opposite: Enjoying the view in the late
evening sun.

Detail of the rigging on a tall ship. Opposite: **Linger on
the deck and enjoy the sunshine.**

The restaurant serves up culinary tours de force daily, accompanied by the finest wines. Especially striking is the informal atmosphere. Anyone in a tie is really overdressed. There is a Captain's Dinner, as on nearly all cruise ships, but here no one turns up in a dinner jacket or evening dress. It is simply not expected. What counts on board the *Star Clipper* is real sailing and everything that goes with it. If you want, you can help the crew keep the ship on course by sighting the sun, standing at the helm, or helping to hoist the sails. But if you don't want to help, no problem. You can simply sip your cocktail of the day, lounge in a comfortable deck chair on one of the three decks, listen to the babble of the water and the gentle creaking of the teak deck, and enjoy the sultry breeze.

This style of cruising is much sportier than the norm – not only because you can actually help sail, but also because there are a lot of water sports facilities on board. If you fancy water-skiing, for example, a quick word with one of the sports team is all it takes and they will arrange it. It is even possible to gain a PADI diving certificate during your cruise. As the four-master is relatively small (the ship carries a maximum of 120 passengers), the atmosphere on board is genuinely intimate. You will quickly get to know most passengers and crew. You can approach the captain at any time, and in the evening he usually comes to the deck bar to drink his coffee

Enjoying the sun, wind and sea. Opposite: The *Star Clipper* anchored at Tobago Cays, where guests can enjoy the clear waters.

and chat, something that does not happen on a regular cruise ship.

Sailing through the Caribbean, the days have begun to run into each other in a delightfully relaxing way. St Lucia, Bequia and Grenada are just a few of the picturesque islands we have visited. Some people make excursions; others try water sports or simply relax on board. At Tobago Cays, the crew had a surprise in store for us. The ship anchored in a small, secluded bay (the relatively shallow draft of tall ships means they can reach places inaccessible to bigger cruise ships). And while we were transported to an uninhabited island in a tender (a shuttle boat that sails between a ship at anchor and the shore) to go snorkelling, water-skiing or diving, the crew unexpectedly came over to provide us with a complete barbecue for lunch. Tables, chairs, crates full of food and drink – everything was hauled onto the beach to give us guests a wonderfully unforgettable afternoon.

Mikael Krafft obviously enjoys his ship. As a young boy, the Swede lived near to the famous shipyard of Plyms in Saltsjöbaden. There, he listened to nostalgic tales from shipbuilders about the romance of big sailing ships. When he was given a small sail boat for his tenth birthday, there was no stopping him. He stole away in his boat to visit the *Pommern* in secret, a clipper moored as a museum ship in Aland. Unseen, he climbed on board and was deeply moved by the magnificence of the ship. He promised himself that one day he would build a ship like that.

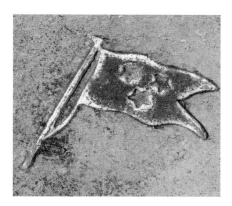

Left: **Well-trained sailors make sure the ropes are neatly stowed.**

Several years later, after graduating in maritime law, Krafft found himself working in ship brokering. He bought a small but solid shipping company and built up an empire of transport ships. But the dream of building a tall ship continued to eat away at him. The only problem was the cost: designing and building a ship does not come cheaply. Then Krafft had a simple yet ingenious idea: the cost of building one ship would always be uneconomical, but if he were to build two identical ships they would be much cheaper per unit. And this was how the identical twins *Star Clipper* and *Star Flyer* came into being.

Krafft, not one to rest on his laurels, then faced up to the challenge of an even bigger childhood dream. As a young boy, he had had a photo of the *Preussen* above his bed. This completely square-rigged five-masted tall ship dominated the world's seas between 1902 and 1910 as the fastest sail ship ever, until it was rammed by a steamboat that had misjudged its speed. If that ship could only be brought to life again…. With two magnificent tall ships already under his belt, Krafft set about designing and building a third. The result was the *Royal Clipper*, the biggest sailing ship in the world. The design of the 133-metre (436-foot) ship is closely based on the legendary *Preussen*. She has forty-two sails with a total surface area of around 5,000 square metres (18,940 square feet) and can carry 227 passengers. Everywhere she goes she makes an impression, just like the *Preussen* a hundred years ago.

Freight ships
An age-old tradition

Those who enjoy the peace and serenity of sailing on the sea, who want to observe the varied life of a modern sailor from close up, and who shy away from organized activities and crowds of people, would do well to consider a cruise on a freight ship.

In actual fact, passenger travel on board modern freight ships is a continuation of a centuries-old tradition: before the arrival of cruise ships, it was perfectly normal for freight ships to offer accommodation for a few passengers. When the ships of the Dutch East India Company took passengers along on their journeys to Asia in the 17th century, these paying guests received preferential treatment: they were given the best cabins and ate with the officers.

Today, most freighters that carry passengers on board have room for a maximum of twelve people, guaranteeing that you will never feel part of a tourist horde. That low figure is due to the fact that international shipping law requires a doctor to be on board if there are more than twelve passengers. First aid is of course always available, but it's worth bearing in mind that you need to be reasonably healthy if you want undertake such a cruise. Most shipping companies require so-called deviation insurance, which covers their expenses if a ship has to divert to a nearby port because a passenger needs unexpected medical assistance. This can incur enormous costs which are not covered by regular insurance.

Large ports such as Rotterdam, above, are always full of activity.

The atmosphere on board a freight ship is quite unlike that on a regular cruise ship. Out on the open sea without an entertainment programme, you are soon thrown upon your own resources and those of your fellow passengers. For those who are able to amuse themselves, this is very relaxing. The cabins are comfortable, with their own shower, toilet and air-conditioning, and are not inferior to those of the average cruise ship. They are often former

Storage tanks and containers. If you travel on a containership, bear in mind that the view from your cabin can at times be blocked by piles of containers.

officers' cabins: increasing automation has led to a big drop in shipping personnel numbers in recent years, and the surplus cabins are now turned into profit by hiring them out. These cabins are usually on the upper deck and have a window, though on containerships it is not unusual for the view to be temporarily blocked by piles of containers.

Most freight ships have a small fitness room on board and there might be a swimming pool or sauna, or both. There is always television and the opportunity to watch films on video or DVD. But beyond that it is up to the guest to decide how he or she wants to spend their time. You might sit on the deck with a book and enjoy the view, chat or have a game with the other passengers, or stroll around the ship. Friendships forged with other passengers can often prove long-lasting; after all, what sort of people make such a voyage? Well, almost by definition they are adventurous, self-reliant, independent and open to new experiences. They are also often people who can afford to spend a long time away, for example because they are retired, have their own businesses, or are teachers or students perhaps rejoining family in another part of the world. However, the length of the journey is up to you: it can vary from three or four days to a hundred or so days for a cruise around the world. And there are routes in all different parts of the globe to choose between.

Passengers certainly need to be flexible, especially when travelling on a tramp ship. These ships sometimes do not know where they are due to collect their next load until they are en route. Even on scheduled services, where destinations are fixed, arrival and departure times can change.

Most freighters that carry passengers are scheduled service ships, enabling passengers to research and read up on the route and destinations in advance. After a few days on the open sea, the approach to a port and then mooring alongside the quay are always fascinating, and the possibility of exploring a town or city is more than welcome. The time that a ship spends in the port is kept to a minimum: after all, time is money. A containership will on average spend between six and twenty-four hours loading and unloading in a modern port, while other freighters can sometimes spend a few days in a port. Bear in mind that these ships will be calling at industrial ports that are usually quite far from the town or city centre: after all, these are not luxury cruise ships docking at a cruise terminal situated for the convenience of tourists. As always on such a journey, a flexible and adventurous attitude is essential. But the contrast between the peace at sea and the hustle and bustle in port is always exciting, and docking at a working port only adds to that.

Huge hoists and cranes are vital
equipment for the work of every port.

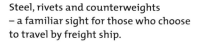
Steel, rivets and counterweights
– a familiar sight for those who choose
to travel by freight ship.

Another significant advantage of a cruise on a freight ship is of course the price, which is usually half or even a third of that of a normal cruise, bringing even a world cruise into the realms of affordability for many more people. Without a programme of organized entertainments, mealtimes are the only fixed point of the day. Passengers eat with the officers and the food is always good quality. The cost of three meals a day is included in the price of the journey, and there is usually a glass of good wine served with lunch and dinner. The galley is open most of the time for snacks, and alcoholic and non-alcoholic drinks are available at duty-free prices. Don't expect any captain's dinners or other special festivities. Gentlemen can leave their dinner jackets and ties at home, and ladies can forget the cocktail dress. There is no dress code: people just wear whatever they are comfortable in. As a passenger you feel a genuine connection with the international crew, despite the fact that you are on holiday and the others are mostly working. This is real modern sea life, and it feels a privilege to be part of it.

3

Fascinating routes

Next to the water in Barcelona there is a column bearing a statue of the explorer Christopher Columbus. He points resolutely out to sea, as if to say: 'There lies the answer!'

Columbus, who was born in Italy in 1451, was convinced that there was a western route to India, and he longed for an opportunity to prove it. His efforts to seek financial support for such a voyage came to nothing at the Portuguese and British courts, but eventually the King of Spain agreed to help him realize his dream. The rest is history. A journey full of adventures climaxed with a near-mutiny by the crew, just before the cry went up of 'Land ahoy!' While Columbus thought he had discovered India – and hence the use ever after of the word Indian to describe the indigenous population – he was actually setting foot in the Americas.

Nowadays such navigational mistakes would be unthinkable. Thanks to modern technology and satellite navigation, cruise ships know exactly where they are to within a few metres, even when they are in the middle of the ocean. But this does not mean to say that there are no exciting or adventurous routes left – on the contrary. Even a transatlantic crossing still has a great deal of magic, and allows you to feel more like a traveller than a tourist. There really is no better way to cross the ocean, especially when journeying westwards from Southampton to New York, when because you are travelling through five time zones, you get an extra hour every night. That means you arrive in the Big Apple nicely relaxed. It's an advantage not to be underestimated.

Opposite: **Anyone who goes on a world cruise will visit many famous buildings. Pictured is the Blue Mosque in Istanbul.**

Many people dream of cruising around the world. This is no everyday journey. In fact for most it is a once-in-a-lifetime experience. Even then, cost can be an obstacle, but there is always the option of doing part of a world cruise. Alternatively, you could cruise to a particular destination. The best example remains the Caribbean, the most popular cruise ship destination in the world. The region is of course extremely well-suited to holidays: sun, sea and numerous islands to visit. But don't imagine – as I once did myself – that one island is pretty much the same as the next. Far from it. One of the reasons cruising in this region is so attractive is that each island has its own distinctive atmosphere, culture and history. Another classic cruise destination is French Polynesia. More remote and relatively isolated, this breathtakingly beautiful area has fewer tourists than the Caribbean, making it *the* dream destination for many people.

Opposite and below: **Shanghai by night. This dazzling city is a favourite port of call during world cruises.**

Sun, sea and sand

The Caribbean region is the most popular cruise destination in the world. Nowhere else welcomes quite so many cruise ships, but the large number of islands means there are ample ports of call to host them all.

The seas around the Caribbean have always been busy, even in days gone by. Though in the past these waters were also notorious for the pirate ships that preyed on regular ship traffic. The numerous bays meant that the pirates had ideal hiding places from which to launch surprise attacks. Blackbeard is one of the most legendary pirates who terrorized the Caribbean region, hijacking around twenty ships between 1716 and 1718. An Englishman whose real name was Edward Teach, tradition has it that he was a tall, imposing figure who would stick burning matches under the rim of his hat and in his huge black beard during raids to intimidate his victims. He and his men would board a ship and seize everything of value, including food, liquor and weapons. If they met with any resistance, they would slaughter all aboard.

Caribbean waters are much calmer nowadays, at least where pirates, hijackers and buccaneers are

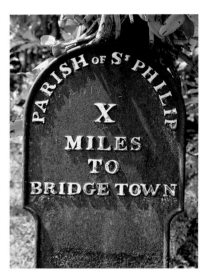

Previous pages: **Souvenir shells at Tobago Cays.**
These pages: **The Caribbean is all about sunshine,
clear seas, sumptuous beaches and joie de vivre.**

concerned. As far as shipping goes, it is the numerous cruise ships that provide the customary hustle and bustle. One of Blackbeard's former hiding places – St Thomas, one of the United States Virgin Islands – is now the most visited port of call in the world. It can, and regularly does, accommodate up to eight mega-ships. The island is then overrun by up to 20,000 people, most of them in search of a bargain in the popular tax-free shops, which are also a major attraction on the islands of Aruba and St Maarten.

However, the Caribbean region has a lot more to offer than just cheap shopping. Magnificent white sandy beaches, azure seas and lots of opportunities for water sports are what make it so popular. The splendid underwater scenery is irresistible to snorkellers and divers: some of the best diving locations in the world are here. On Bonaire, a small island near Curaçao, yellow rocks at the side of the water indicate the best diving spots. You can simply wade into the water wearing your diving equipment and plunge in. No boat necessary! Onshore, you will see many pick-up trucks driving around with diving bottles in the back. And of course, the laid-back attitude of the islands' inhabitants is hugely seductive to a great many holidaymakers coming from the hectic West. For anyone who has ever visited Jamaica, the words 'yeah man, no problem!' will ever after be music to their ears. Lots of cruises to the Caribbean leave from Florida (where Miami is a real cruise hub) or Puerto Rico. In order to give their passengers an unforgettable day, some cruise companies even have their own private island, where you can swim, sunbathe and enjoy all different types of water sports as well as a delicious barbecue on the beach.

The Caribbean region, sandwiched between North and South America, is named after one of the indigenous tribes that lived here when the first Europeans arrived. These Caribs were famously aggressive. They migrated across from South America and drove away many of the original inhabitants of the islands, the Arawaks, with violence. At the beginning of the 16th century, the Spaniards built settlements in the area: first in Hispaniola (the island

that today comprises the Dominican Republic and Haiti), then in Cuba, Jamaica and Puerto Rico. Remains from those early colonial times, such as the fort of San Juan on Puerto Rico, are fascinating to visit.

The Spanish colonists promptly enslaved the original inhabitants, setting them to work in gold and silver mines on the South American mainland. Ships returned to Europe laden with gold, silver and precious stones. This traffic attracted many pirates of different nationalities, and numerous Spanish vessels were seized or ended up at the bottom of the ocean.

During the 17th century, when the power of the Spanish went into a gradual decline, France, Great Britain and Holland stepped in and claimed entire islands as their own imperial property. It was Dutch colonists who first introduced some 1,630 sugar canes from Brazil to the Caribbean region, establishing the first plantations on Barbados.

Sunset in Barbados, time for a stroll along the beach.

Right and below: **Colourful souvenirs on sale in Antigua.** Far right: **Bougainvillea grows abundantly in the Caribbean.** Opposite: **A watchtower on the old Spanish fort of San Cristóbal in San Juan on Puerto Rico.** Following pages: **A bobbing boat in St Vincent.**

They quickly proved to be enormously lucrative and soon the whole area was full of plantations. Processing the sugar cane was extremely labour-intensive and to meet the huge demand for labour, millions of African slaves were transported across the Atlantic. This cruel practice was not ended until the 19th century, and it is of course the reason that the largest proportion of the population of these islands is of African origin.

Even today, France, Britain and Holland still retain colonies in the Caribbean region. On these islands and others that have long since won their independence, the influence of the former European rulers remains apparent. On Barbados, for example, where the British held sway for 340 years, cricket is still a very popular sport and afternoon tea is served every day. A good example of the rich mixture of influences in the region is Papiamento, a language spoken on the Netherlands-owned ABC islands (Aruba, Bonaire and Curaçao). Its vocabulary includes elements contributed by African slaves, Dutch traders, Spanish missionaries and local Indians.

Sugar cane is the basis of the most famous drink to come out of the Caribbean, rum. Barbados, Jamaica, Guadeloupe and Martinique in particular are famous for their fine rum, which is a key export product. Holiday-makers in the Caribbean will soon become acquainted with this spirit, as rum cocktails are a good alternative to wine, which is not produced here.

In fact no cruise in the Caribbean would be complete without having enjoyed a rum punch, piña colada or Cuba libre.

The classic among cruises

World cruises
and transatlantic crossings

Spending weeks or months on a voyage of discovery to the most interesting places
on earth – who wouldn't jump at the chance?

A genuine world cruise remains one of the ultimate and most inspiring journeys a person can make.

Clockwise from top left: **One of the statues in St Peter's Square in Rome; The gondolas of Venice; The dome of St Peter's Basilica in Rome; A view of Florence.** Previous pages: **Such marvellous sky and seascapes are a regular sight during a world cruise.**

A **world cruise is** a complete circuit of the earth in a fixed direction – don't be fooled by those shipping companies that incorrectly use the term 'world cruise' to denote a route between two different parts of the world. A genuine world cruise is the classic cruising experience; indeed it has been the icing on the cruise cake for nearly a century. Of course, being away from home for such a long time requires good preparation. If you are going to be on the same ship for many weeks or months, you need to be sure you are going to feel comfortable on it. Of at least equal importance is the route the ship is going to sail, the ports of call and how long you will spend in them. Most journeys go in a westerly direction, which means that when you change time zones you have the relaxing bonus of gaining an hour. (Sailing eastwards means the opposite: there will be numerous 23-hour days.) It is not just passengers but also ship owners that have to plan world cruises very carefully. When a ship is en route for so long, it is of course feasible that something will break at any time and have to be repaired. Consequently, all sorts of replacement parts for the most diverse pieces of equipment have to be taken along, just in case repairs are necessary. World cruises entail many whole days being spent at sea. But for example, over the course of a world cruise lasting 108 days, the *Queen Elizabeth 2* will generally call at more than forty different ports, staying for a few days at some places. It's the perfect combination of relaxation and exploration.

A full world cruise will often take as much as half a year. But if you can't spare that long, most ships also offer the opportunity to sail part of the route only. Shipping companies deploy ships in different areas depending on the season: thus ships that sail in the Caribbean between September and April are transferred to European waters in the remaining months of the year. You can even travel on a ship when it is being repositioned in this

Statue of the reclining Buddha, offerings, and the tower of Phra Sri Ratana Chedi, all in Bangkok.

way, creating interesting route possibilities. The length of this sort of journey varies from a week and a half to around three weeks.

Alternatively you could consider a transatlantic crossing, a cruise of sorts that is a continuation of a tradition that has lasted many years. Prior to the introduction of the aeroplane as a means of mass transportation, this was the only way to reach the United States from Europe, and in the early 20th century, several shipping companies offered a regular service, including the Holland America Line. Nowadays, Cunard is the only company that provides passenger crossings on a regular basis. The *Queen Mary 2*, which took over the route from the *QE2* in 2004, was built to withstand the occasionally harsh weather on the Atlantic Ocean. Indeed, on its very first transatlantic crossing from Southampton to New York in April 2004, it received a real baptism of fire – or rather a baptism of water – when it was faced with waves of between 10 and 14 metres (33 to 46 feet). The ship did not flinch and completed the journey, partly thanks to its stabilizers, in the planned six days and in reasonable comfort.

But if a world cruise remains the ultimate cruise, then there is no finer way to do it than on the ship *The World,* which sails around the world continuously at a very gentle pace. This is no ordinary cruise ship, since here it is possible to rent or buy apartments on board. Her owners describe this as the only private sailing community in the world. The ship has 165 apartments, ranging from a one-room studio with basic kitchenette to a three-bedroom suite with a surface area of 300 square metres (3,330 square feet) and a private jet pool on the veranda. Because these spaces amount

A warm reception awaits you in Ho Chi Minh City, formerly Saigon. Right: Colourful lanterns in a display window in Da Nang in Vietnam, a popular port of call during a world cruise.

to a second home for many owners, they are not permanently inhabited, so many apartments are available for hire. There are on average between 150 and 200 guests on board, plus a 250-strong crew, including a full medical staff. The minimum rental period is six nights.

Those who do not want to cook for themselves can choose to dine in one of the four speciality restaurants which the ship has to offer. An appetite for literature can be satisfied in the extensive library. *The World* has a spa and other facilities that can be found on standard cruise ships, such as two swimming pools, a golf simulator and a tennis court. Classical concerts are staged in the auditorium, and it is possible to take lessons in a variety of subjects such as dance, photography or music. There is also a full-time professional golf instructor on board, and The World Golf Club provides the opportunity to play golf in each port of call, including some of the world's most famous golf courses. *The World* wants to distance itself from normal cruise ships by creating an atmosphere that makes guests feel as if they are sailing on board their own private yacht. One of many innovations this inspired is the 'Call a Chef' facility. Would you like to eat with friends in your own apartment but don't fancy cooking? A chef from one of the restaurants will come on request and prepare your chosen menu in your own apartment. The ship stays in port for an average of two to three days, giving you plenty of time to explore your surroundings. And just like on normal cruise ships, it is possible to book excursions from *The World*. Discovering the world on board a ship that really does feel like home – what could possibly be nicer?

Travelling in a westerly direction means
that when you change time zones you have the
relaxing bonus of gaining an hour.

Paradise
on earth

Say 'French Polynesia' and you may get a slightly blank response.

Say 'Tahiti' and your listener is likely to be flooded with visions of

a tropical paradise: beautiful beaches, exotic beauties and tattooed men.

The idyllic beaches and crystal-clear waters of French Polynesia.

Tahiti is the largest and best known of the French Polynesian archipelago. This comprises 118 different islands divided into five distinct groups which together spread over an area of the South Pacific Ocean the size of Western Europe. Tahiti is one of the group known as the Society Islands, strikingly green islands that also include Bora Bora, Moorea, Huahine and Raiatea. There's no better way to get acquainted with them than by cruise ship: island groups are extraordinarily suited to this type of holiday. Most of the Society Islands are surrounded by a lagoon, a relatively shallow area of sea between the island and an encircling barrier reef. These peaceful areas are turquoise in colour and contrast beautifully with the deep blue of the ocean. Openings in the barrier reef allow cruise ships to enter and depart as they sail from island to island.

In truth, anyone who comes to French Polynesia primarily for the beaches is likely to be disappointed: unlike in the Caribbean or Asia, you will not find endlessly long white beaches fringed with palm trees here. What beaches there are have either been artificially constructed by hotels, or they are on motus,

small islands of sand in the lagoons. Some resorts are to be found on motus, and it is always possible to get a small boat to drop you there and collect you later. On the other hand, the water in French Polynesia is startlingly clear, and the wonderful lagoons are perfect for snorkelling and diving. The clear water also makes pearl culturing a lucrative business. Black pearls in particular are a speciality of this area; after tourism French Polynesia today depends economically on trade in pearls and related products such as mother-of-pearl.

In the 18th century, European explorers returned home with spectacular stories about Tahiti. The English ship the *Dolphin*, under the command of Samuel Wallis, was the first European ship to anchor at Tahiti when she moored at Matavai Bay in 1767. She was welcomed by thousands of seemingly enthusiastic inhabitants who surrounded the ship in hundreds of canoes. However, the crew's delight soon turned into fear as stones rained down on the *Dolphin*. When the Tahitians tried to board the ship, Wallis gave the order to aim the cannons. A bloodbath ensued, and a few days later the crew mounted an action that

A boat bobs on the water.
Opposite: **Anchored in Cook's Bay in Moorea.**

destroyed dozens of canoes belonging to the native inhabitants. Rather improbably, however, peace was restored and a lively trade ensued. The Tahitians were unfamiliar with iron, and knives and nails were eagerly exchanged for food – and more. For as the crew of the *Dolphin* soon found out, the native Tahitians had particularly free morals. In exchange for a simple nail, which could be used to make a fish hook, the women would offer sexual services. Accounts by later visitors, such as the Frenchman Louis Antoine de Bougainville and the famous English explorer James Cook, told of beautiful, half-naked women and men who danced provocatively and were very free with sex. Paris and London were fascinated by these stories, and an exotic myth was born that has lured many adventurers and artists over the years – among them Paul Gauguin – and continues to entice travellers today.

It was Captain Cook who mapped the Polynesian region precisely in the course of three voyages of discovery. One of the most beautiful and well-known bays in the archipelago is named after him: Cook's Bay on Moorea. But it was an episode that took place a few years after Cook's voyages that forms many people's image of Tahiti, namely the true story of the mutiny on the *Bounty*. In April 1789, Fletcher Christian led a mutiny on the English ship the *Bounty*,

A colourful shawl and a local beauty.
Left: **The water in French Polynesia is unbelievably clear.**

which was under the command of Captain William Bligh, a young officer who had served as a navigator on Cook's voyages in the South Pacific. The *Bounty* had set off for Tahiti at the end of 1787 in search of breadfruit plants to be transported to the Caribbean, where the nourishing fruits would feed the slaves of the British colonies. They found what they were looking for, but on the return journey, which was taking much longer than planned, mutiny broke out among the crew. The captain and eighteen crew members loyal to him were set adrift on the ocean in a basic boat while Christian took the *Bounty* and headed back to Tahiti.

Bligh was by all accounts a cruel man but he was also an outstanding sailor and navigator, and after a journey of around 5,800 kilometres (3,600 miles) he eventually reached Timor, from where he made the return journey to England in a comfortable fashion. Christian's group split in the meantime, and the rebel leader departed with eight of his men and nineteen native inhabitants (six men, twelve women and a child) to uninhabited Pitcairn Island, where they established a community whose descendants still live there today. Those mutineers who remained on Tahiti received an unexpected visit. The English ship the *Pandora,* under the command of Captain Edwards, came for them in 1791 to bring them to trial

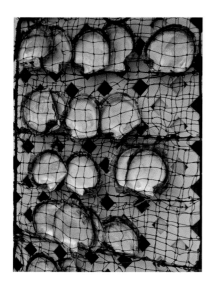

Shells hang drying in a pearl farm. Right: **Characteristic Polynesian houses on stilts, here on Tahiti.** Following pages: **Sailing from Moorea to Raiatea.**

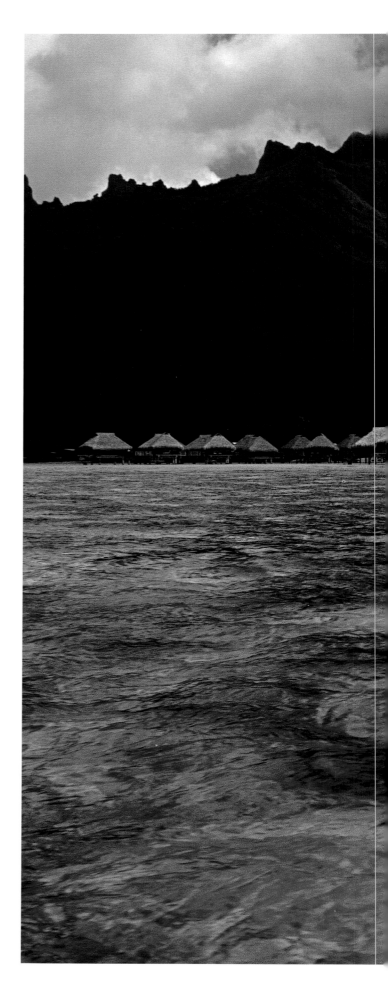

in London. Four of the mutineers died en route during a storm; of the men who survived, six were hanged and three were cleared.

Men in the Polynesian region are believed to have sported their famous tattoos since 1500 BC. An even more intriguing detail of Polynesian civilization is that male transvestites are an accepted social phenomenon; they appear in the reports of the very first European explorers. Known as mahus or, in more recent times, rae rae, these boys would be brought up as girls and would behave and dress as women. As adults they played a valued role in society. Traditionally a boy would be designated as a mahu by his parents, usually because there were no daughters in the family to help the mother, and in a society where work was strictly designated as 'male' or 'female', it made more sense to raise a boy as a girl than to expect a boy to perform female tasks. Today the legacy of this tradition is tolerance: boys are free to follow the path they choose, and homosexuality and transvestism are unproblematic. It's just one more fascinating detail that makes French Polynesia such a wonderful and intriguing place to visit.

4

Nature and expedition cruises

Many of the world's most beautiful natural destinations are best reached by cruise or expedition ship. The Galapagos Islands are a perfect example: there are hotels there, but if you want to visit several islands (and you really should), a ship is so much more convenient. Most of the land area is protected under strict conservation laws, which stipulate that the delicate flora and fauna can only be visited in the company of a guide. An expedition or nature cruise will organize this for you. Exploring during the day, then relaxing on the ship in the evening, allowing all the images and impressions to sink in, and also deepening your knowledge of the ecosystem and geography of your chosen destination by listening to on-board lectures – a cruise can really make your experience complete.

Such nature cruises are invariably accompanied by experts such as biologists, zoologists and geologists. Their lectures are often the only entertainment on board: you will not find any casinos, theatres or other organized amusements here. But that's not a problem with the nature-lovers who choose this sort of cruising experience. Passengers will often be handed a notebook containing detailed information on the animals and landscape they are visiting, as well as space for adding their own notes and so creating a personal journal by which to remember their trip.

The expedition leader will supervise any excursions. During my own expedition to Antarctica, the leaders (two brothers) turned out to be old hands. Each of them had made more than 150 trips to the frozen continent and had plenty of unbeatably colourful stories to tell.

Expedition ships are smaller than cruise ships and have a shallower draft, allowing them to reach many more places. If sailing in icy regions they

Opposite: **Boating on a tributary of the Amazon in South America.**

will often have a strengthened bow. They carry Zodiacs, inflatable rubber boats with outboard engines that are used to carry passengers onto land. In Antarctica, where there are no ports, landing stages or piers, these are indispensable. And they have the added benefit of making you feel like a real explorer.

Besides Antarctica, other popular cold destinations include the Arctic, Greenland and Alaska, which with its rugged landscape and spectacular glaciers (there are at least sixteen in Glacier Bay National Park) is very popular with cruise ships. Some cruise companies offer passengers pre- or post-cruise accommodation in their hotels and lodges in Alaska. Such companies also have their own coaches and train services. Nature is big business in Alaska.

There are plenty of nature cruises to other parts of the world too. You could take a trip along the Amazon in South America or go dragon-watching on Komodo Island in Asia. You might visit the Chilean fjords, Australia's Great Barrier Reef, or take a cruise around South Africa to encounter the country's magnificent wildlife. An expedition cruise is the ideal way to see some of the most spectacular flora, fauna and scenery on the planet.

Opposite: **Africa provides a number of popular cruise destinations.**
Below: **Sunlight on a palm leaf in Florida.**

The last
Antarctica
wilderness

The existence of
Antarctica was not confirmed until the 19th century. People had speculated about the possibility
of a continent at the South Pole for millennia, but extreme weather conditions
meant that it remained undiscovered right into the modern era.

R enewed interest in the possibility of a southern land mass was sparked in February 1819 when seal hunter William Smith reported that there was a large seal population in the South Shetland Islands. These islands lie just off the western coast of the Antarctic Peninsula. In those days, seal hunting was big business, and people were eager to know what lay beyond the islands. In 1823, the Englishman James Weddell sailed further south than anyone had ever done before. The challenge was set to reach the real South Pole.

It was later Pole explorers such as Scott, Shackleton and Amundsen that gave the continent a face and an unforgettable story: by means of the relatively new invention of photography, but also through the journals in which they recorded their adventures. The first person to reach the South Pole, on 14 December 1911, was the Norwegian Captain Roald Amundsen. The English Captain Robert F. Scott was en route to the same destination at the same time, but Amundsen was much more efficient. With clothing made of reindeer skin, and well-trained huskies, he reached the South Pole eight days ahead of his expedition schedule. Scott, who was travelling with a larger group and ponies, slipped behind schedule. The ponies sank into the snow and had to be put down, leaving the men to pull the sleds bearing their provisions themselves. When they finally reached the South Pole, they discovered that Amundsen had been there before them. Disillusioned, they turned back, but winter set in and they never

succeeded in reaching their home
base. Scott's entire party eventually
froze to death.

In the extreme conditions of
Antarctica, safety is paramount,
even for today's high-tech cruise

A chinstrap penguin defies the cold and
enjoys the view. Previous pages: the
Antarctic Dream is parked in the ice and
the crew goes off to investigate.

ships. Caroline, a 34-year-old woman from Liverpool, was taken by surprise when she joined an expedition ship to Antarctica:

And I thought I was going on a cruise… soon I realize it is truly more of an expedition. The mandatory Antarctica weatherproof boots and jackets were a hint, then there was the serious emergency drill, with serious life jackets and serious lifeboats. Our expedition leader is as much of a true sailor as you will ever meet: friendly, authoritarian and complete with schoolbook stern posture and beard (the kind you wanted to marry as a little girl); now that I have listened to the stories of his travels, I have readjusted my expectations and look forward to the travel south even more!

Antarctica is the most southerly destination that can be reached by cruise ship. It is also probably the most spectacular. In summer, the rocks and permanent ice on this continent occupy 14 million square kilometres (5.5 million square miles); in winter the surface doubles as a result of ice formation, extending over an area bigger than Europe. It is a place of extremes. The lowest temperature ever recorded on earth was here: minus 89° Celsius (minus 128° Fahrenheit). This is the windiest continent and, improbable though it may sound,

the driest. Around 90 per cent of the planet's ice is here, and thus almost 70 per cent of its freshwater supplies. If all of the ice in Antarctica were to melt, the sea level across the whole of the earth would rise by 85 metres (280 feet).

A chinstrap penguin poses for the camera. Top: **Calm water in a bay.**

The differences between here and the opposite end of the earth, the Arctic, are greater than you might think. While Antarctica is a continent surrounded by sea, the Arctic is a frozen sea surrounded by continents. The North Pole is just one metre above sea level, while the average height of Antarctica is 2,180 metres (7,150 feet). The Arctic is home to reindeer, wolves, polar bears and foxes as well as sea mammals, but there are no land mammals in Antarctica, only sea mammals. And at minus 18° Celsius (minus 0.4° Fahrenheit), the average temperature at the North Pole is much higher than at the South Pole, where the average temperature is minus 50° Celsius (minus 58° Fahrenheit).

Crossing the churning Southern Ocean can be a challenge. These are some of the world's stormiest seas, and it is only a lucky few who escape a bout of seasickness. In my case I fought it by allowing the ship's doctor to drug me with a tablet that put me to sleep for twelve hours straight. After that I was able to appreciate the great food – quite unexpected here on the bottom of the earth – and the mandatory leisure. From the first day aboard there was no cellphone network coverage, no communication possible with home or work – these days you have to travel a very long way to really get away. My journal captures the sheer delight and wonder I felt as we approached the Antarctic continent.

My first iceberg! At 5.00 a.m., the voice of the expedition leader wakes me with the promise of sunshine and icebergs; I am up and dressed and on deck in minutes. What a thrill! It's like sailing through a movie set or a living postcard,

*the most surrealistic scenery I have
ever come across; nothing but blue
sky, sunshine, and a flat sea with
immense ice cubes floating around,
as many and as blue as you could
ever imagine.*

Today I set foot on the Antarctic continent, in perfect weather conditions. Not cold at all. Some dark clouds that give a feeling of wilderness, and patches of blue blue sky. The ice master sailed the ship straight into a stretch of ice, allowing us to climb right on to the frozen water, and we got to walk about in this fantastic landscape like true explorers. The scenery was unbelievably beautiful, icebergs like great abstract sculptures drifting in the water, 3,000-metre (10,000-foot) mountaintops towering behind, and all covered in a thick layer of snow.

It feels as if I have landed on a faraway planet inhabited by penguins. They are the most entertaining animals; just looking at them puts a smile on your face. It is the way they walk, or rather wiggle,

and their friendly appearance. They are such fun to watch! And they all seem to making up for a lost childhood dream of being a famous model, eagerly posing for pictures, showing themselves from every angle in every possible – and seemingly impossible – position.

Following the signing of the international Antarctic Treaty in 1959, there is now permanent surveillance in the Antarctic region. The twelve original signatories (Argentina, Australia, Belgium, Great Britain, Chile, France, Japan, New Zealand, Norway, the Soviet

These pages: **The fantastic forms of the icebergs are fascinating; some are like floating works of art. Passengers of the** *Antarctic Dream* **are brought ashore in a Zodiac.** Following pages: **An imposing iceberg floats by. In the background are the peaks of the Transantarctic Mountain range.**

Union, South Africa and the United States) wanted to prevent the continent falling victim to competing superpower claims or being used for military or nuclear testing, and to ensure that its environment was fully protected. Since 1959, forty-four more countries have acceded to the treaty, which forbids military activity, refuses national claims to land, and guarantees free access to scientific research. There are now more than fifty bases housing around five thousand personnel undertaking a wide variety of research. But their presence makes almost no impact on this vast continent, with its icy landscape of dramatic beauty and extraordinary variety of marine and sealife. Antarctica really is the last pristine wilderness on the planet.

Darwin's

Galapagos Islands laboratory

The Galapagos Islands have been described as a 'Garden of Eden in the Calm of the Ocean'. The naturalist and explorer Charles Darwin spent five weeks here in 1835, and the research he carried out was to provide the foundation for his theory of evolution.

The Galapagos Islands were discovered in 1535 by the Bishop of Panama Thomás de Berlanga, who went off course on his way to Peru and came upon the archipelago by accident. His account of the rugged, uninhabited volcanic islands included descriptions of the enormous turtles and dragon-like lizards that dwelt there. In 1570, cartographer Abraham Ortelius called the islands 'Insulae de los Galepegos' (Turtle Islands) as a result of de Berlanga's description. Spanish sailors talked of the 'Islas Encantadas' (Enchanted Islands), owing not only to their prehistoric-seeming wildlife but also the unpredictable sea currents and sudden fog banks that often made it look as though the islands were floating on the surface of the sea.

For the next two centuries, the only humans to come here were pirates and buccaneers seeking occasional shelter. The giant turtles yielded plenty of tasty meat and the richly loaded Spanish galleons could be easily intercepted from here. The islands provided the perfect base from which to launch sorties.

Even today, the Galapagos Islands are still best visited by ship. The archipelago lies approximately 1,000 kilometres (600 miles) off the coast of Ecuador (to which it belongs), and is made up of dozens of islands of different sizes, just thirteen of which have an area over 10 square kilometres (4 square miles). The total surface area is around 7,800 square kilometres (3,000 square miles). Only a few islands have permanent human inhabitants. Since 1959, the island group has been part of Galapagos National Park, a foundation that oversees and protects their vulnerable ecology. The park authority restricts the numbers of tourists in any one location at a time. Cruise ships have to take this into account when planning their sailing route. There are a number of different cruise ships that sail in the area, and expeditions vary in length from a few days to two weeks. There is an informal atmosphere on board these ships, as is characteristic of all nature and expedition cruises. On board there will always be at least one guide who has been trained by the National Park. These guides give lectures and provide background information on the

Blue-footed boobies can be seen all over the Galapagos Islands.

Tree cacti on Cerro Dragón. Below left: **Marine iguanas warm themselves in the sun.** Below right: **The splendid colours of the land iguana.**

islands, as well as ensuring that guidelines on the protection of flora and fauna are observed once the passengers are on land. Other than in some of the public places on the inhabited islands of Santa Cruz, San Cristóbal, Isabela and Floreana, it is forbidden to visit the islands or go on an exploratory expedition without a guide.

There are few places in the world where you can find so many unique animal and plant varieties concentrated in such a small area. Most of these drifted or flew over from the mainland over the course of millennia, then continued to evolve in isolation from their parent species. It was the remarkable distinctiveness of the flora and fauna here that set Darwin thinking. He was famously fascinated by the so-called Galapagos finches. On one island he observed that these had large thick beaks for cracking nuts and seeds, on another they had thin beaks for eating fruit and flowers, while on yet another they had small beaks and ate insects. He realized that the birds had physically adapted to be better able to exploit the food available in their isolated territory over the years. The discovery that animals change over time in order to thrive in their environment became the basis of the theory of evolution by natural selection. In 1859, Darwin published the results of his research and reflections in the book *On the Origin of Species*. It is hard to grasp now just how shocking his theories were back then – so shocking they seemed almost criminal. They contradicted the Genesis creation story that was still generally accepted in the West, and that underpinned so much of the moral and worldly authority of the Christian Church. Even the captain of the H.M.S. *Beagle*, Robert Fitzroy, in whose company Darwin had sailed around the world as a marine researcher for nearly five years, ended their friendship because of his revolutionary ideas.

Many cruise ships call in at what is by far the largest island in the archipelago, Isla Isabela. This was formed by the fusion of six volcanoes, and is still home to the highest volcanoes in the area: Wolf in the north and Cerro Azul in the south. At the top of another volcano, the Alcedo, thousands of giant turtles live in what is the largest turtle colony on the island, though anyone wishing to visit the Alcedo needs special permission. Another striking

Below: **A lecture on board the *Xpedition*.**
Right: **A young Galapagos turtle.**
Opposite: **A wave breaks on the lava stone rocks.**

inhabitant is the blue-footed booby. This bird was nicknamed 'booby' (which comes from the Spanish for 'stupid fellow') by earlier sailors because it was so completely trusting and saw no danger in the new visitors to its habitat. Alas, boobies often had to pay for their curiosity with their lives, and their numbers at one stage declined to the point of near-extinction, though fortunately their population is now much more secure.

Given that the Galapagos Islands are directly on the equator, one inhabitant you might not expect to find here is the penguin. But a cold current on the western side of the island provides food and ideal living conditions for this small animal. Marine iguanas certainly enjoy this warm location. You regularly see these prehistoric-looking creatures lying around sunbathing: as they do not have a system for regulating their temperature they can become very cold while searching for food in the ocean. Indeed there are dozens of fascinating animal species to marvel at on the Galapagos Islands, many of them extraordinarily tame.

A cruise to the Galapagos Islands is a voyage of discovery to another world – a world of unspoilt nature, where animals do not see mankind as their natural enemy, and where one of the most revolutionary ideas about life on earth was born.

Sailing through the fjords of Chile

South Patagonia

In 1520, the Portuguese explorer Ferdinand Magellan encountered the magnificent fjords of South Patagonia as he made his way down the coast of South America in search of a westward passage to the East. Today you can witness the same spectacular landscape from the comfort of a cruise ship.

South Patagonia is an extraordinarily beautiful place to explore by ship. The region lies at the tip of South America and extends across both Argentina and Chile. Here, the Andes mountain range dives under the water (eventually to re-emerge in Antarctica in the Transantarctic Mountains), creating numerous lakes and fjords, particularly in Chilean Patagonia.

On board one of the cruise ships that sail to Chilean Patagonia, we have not encountered any others since leaving the pick-up point of Punta Arenas (where I saw one cruise ship apart from ours). Unbelievable really, but then there are so many fjords and lakes that there is a wide variety of sailing routes. It is spring, which means it stays light long into the evening. At 11 p.m. last night everyone was standing on deck, armed with cameras and a drink, enjoying the view in the slowly creeping dusk. The moon above the

Fragments of ice from a glacier. Following page: **The moon above the Darwin Plateau.**

glaciers in the Darwin Plateau completed the picture. This morning we disembarked next to a glacier. Enormous pieces of ice break off at regular intervals, landing with a crash. The ground is strewn with chunks of ice. It looks as though we are on another planet.

These stupendous mountains and glaciers cannot have failed to make an impression on Magellan and his men, just as they invariably do on modern-day cruisers like myself. The landscape has barely changed over the five centuries since. Like me, Magellan must have been struck by the curious difference in the mountain peaks, some of which are round as a ball, others sharp and angular. He was probably at a loss to explain this; however, geologists do now have an explanation. The rounded peaks were buried under snow during the last ice age, and their shape was smoothed by the weight and the grating movement of the ice. Sharp summits have always protruded above the ice, where they were more exposed to the elements, and absorbed rain and snowmelt. When this water froze, pieces of rock flew off, leaving multiple jagged peaks.

Ferdinand Magellan was a man with a mission. On the orders of the Spanish king Charles I, he was hoping to discover an as yet unknown westward route to the lands of the East, in particular the Moluccas or Spice Islands. There were many sceptics, but Magellan was convinced such a route existed. On 27 September 1519, he set out as the commander of five ships. The

> The moon above the glaciers in the Darwin Plateau completed the picture.

epic journey was beset by hazards and hardship – mutiny, scurvy, lack of provisions, rough weather. After much roving around, and lots of unrest among the crew, Magellan spied an island with a remarkable number of campfires. These fires had been lit by the original inhabitants, the Selknams, and inspired the Portuguese name Tierra del Fuego (Land of Fire). Eventually, on 1 November 1520, Magellan found what he was looking for: a short-cut from east to west through South America. He originally called this the Strait of 'Todos los Santos' because his crew reached it on All Saints' Day, but it has of course ever after been known in his honour as the Strait of Magellan.

On 27 November Magellan's ship exited the South American continent and reached the South China Sea. Because the waters were calm, he named this ocean the Pacific. The journey continued westwards – the first ever crossing of the Pacific by Europeans. Just five months later, Magellan was killed during a fight with natives on an island that is now part of the Philippines. His ship, the *Victoria* continued on her path to the Moluccas, where she was loaded with precious spices and then set off on the return trip to Spain. She became the first ship to circumnavigate the world.

Magellan not only did not make it back to Europe; he also did not travel as far south as Cape Horn, the southernmost point of the continent. Nearly a century

Images of rugged Cape Horn. The plants here are mainly mosses and grasses. Previous pages: View of the Patagonian mountains from a cruise ship.

later, in 1615, the Dutchman Willem Schouten ventured forth in search of an alternative western route to the East than that discovered by Magellan. With two ships, the *Hoorn* and the *Eendracht*, he left Holland together with Jacobus le Maire. Business interest was again a matter of first importance. The then powerful Dutch East India Company claimed the exclusive right to use the Strait of Magellan. Schouten and le Maire worked for a rival association. Navigating the waters around Tierra del Fuego, they finally found the route they were looking for, to the south of the Strait of Magellan. They called it Le Maire Straat. Then in 1616, their ships rounded the southernmost point of the South American continent, named Kaap Hoorn by Schouten after his birthplace. Triumphant, they set forth for Batavia (present-day Jakarta in Indonesia). No sooner had they arrived, however, than both explorers were arrested by the governor of the Dutch East India Company, accused of having used the Strait of Magellan without authorization. The sailors were taken back to Holland as prisoners. Le Maire died during the journey, and Schouten spent years trying to prove his innocence.

As the southernmost point of the continent, Cape Horn remains a place of huge strategic significance, and it is today the site of a Chilean naval base. However

The monument to dead sailors at Cape Horn. Opposite above: **An albatross in full flight.** Opposite below: **Male and female seals.**

the route around Cape Horn is much less vital to shipping than it once was. It was used a great deal at the time of the tea races and the California gold rush when the stakes were high enough for the risks to be worth it. There was plenty of wind on the route around the Cape, which made it much quicker but also much more dangerous than the sheltered Strait of Magellan. Not until 1914 did the opening of the Panama Canal put an end to this perilous route.

Sailors often refer to Cape Horn as simply 'the Cape', and not without a sense of awe: this region is famous for sudden storms, and shipwrecks abound. When I was there we were lucky with the weather. The sea was calm, and we were able to use Zodiacs to disembark in a bay, from where steps lead up to the highest point of the Cape. It is not until you get to the top that you realize just how extremely windy it is. In fact it is never really calm here. The monument in honour of lost sailors that stands on this point has been made to withstand the very heaviest of storms. The memorial features the silhouette of a flying albatross, since legend has it that sailors who die here are reincarnated in the form of this bird. It is true that there are a great many albatrosses soaring through these southern skies...

5

Interesting ports of call

Approaching a port of call is a high point of any cruise. Of course, the sailing itself is also pleasurable, and many ships have enough distractions and entertainments on board to keep boredom at bay for a lifetime. But still, the destination looming in the distance, growing gradually larger, and the manoeuvres of the ship as it comes alongside the quay provide a wonderful spectacle every time. The hustle and bustle on the dockside, the ship being tied up with huge ropes, and the activities of the crew are all fascinating. And then comes the moment when you cross the gangway or step out of the tender onto dry land and set forth to explore an unfamiliar place, turning back for a moment to view the vessel that has become your temporary new home.

It is often sensible and practical to book an organized excursion, especially if time is short and communication challenging, but whenever possible I still prefer to go out exploring on my own. If you read up on a place beforehand (always worth doing), you will know what you are looking for. There may not be any particular sights to head for. Some destinations lend themselves best to ambling around, perhaps visiting a market, wandering through lanes and alleyways, hunting for a souvenir, followed by lunch in a local restaurant – with a sea view of course. Delightful.

In Havana my ship moored in the very centre of the city, right by the old town. It was a delightful spot from which to stroll around the book market and enjoy this shimmering Caribbean city. In the town of Sorrento in southern Italy, I stumbled upon a wonderful scene of elderly Italians playing cards as I strolled through the narrow shopping alleys. Too good to miss, I snapped a quick photo and reviewed it on my screen later while seated at a pavement café, cappuccino at hand.

Opposite: **The picturesque Italian port town of Portofino is visited by many cruise ships.**

In many big cities, the town centre can be far from where your cruise ship is moored. In this case, taxis offer the best solution – negotiating public transport in a foreign country is always a challenge, so when time is tight, it's generally worth the extra expense. What's more, there is very often added value in the pride so many taxi drivers feel for their hometown and the delight they take in telling you all about it. In Barcelona, I received a free sightseeing tour of some of Gaudí's major buildings once I told my taxi driver I was on a cruise ship and only had one day to see the city. The proud Catalan brought his taxi to a stop in the most impossible places so I could view the buildings, all the while gesticulating wildly and providing a commentary in his heavily accented English. Horn-tooting fellow road-users could not deter him, and he continued talking, beaming at the opportunity, oblivious to the queues of angry drivers building up behind him. His enthusiasm was hugely infectious, and has coloured my own passion for the architect and the city ever since.

Opposite: **Men of Sorrento. Many cruise ships organize trips to Pompeii from here.** Below: **Havana, a shimmering, sweltering cruise destination where ships moor right in the city centre.**

City of Barcelona
Gaudí's
masterpieces

Barcelona is one of Europe's most popular cruise destinations. This is no surprise given just how much this stylish Spanish port city has to offer: a pleasant climate, great shopping, exciting nightlife, outstanding restaurants and an abundance of culture.

The man who has left the single most defining mark on the Catalan capital is the visionary architect Antoni Gaudí. His works are to be seen across the entire city, and they continue to draw admirers from around the world. One spectacular example is the famous residential complex Casa Milà, with its undulating windows and balconies, endless sculptural decoration and splendid roof terrace. Then there is the Sagrada Família, the cathedral on which the 74-year-old Gaudí was working when he died in 1926 – knocked down by a tram while crossing the street, he died from his injuries three days later. This is still under construction today, but you can visit the site, climb some of the towers and in the museum view models of what the building should eventually look like.

And there is Park Güell. This, the second biggest park in Barcelona, is built on a hillside in the northeast of the city. It stands like a huge, colourful work of art – a sculpture of gigantic proportions. It was commissioned by Eusebi Güell, a great admirer and patron of Gaudí. However, Güell's original conception was of no mere park – this was to be an entire private residential area for the well-to-do bourgeois of Barcelona, enclosed and protected from the city

A view of Barcelona from Park Güell.

Gaudí used the rocks and boulders excavated from the site as building materials for Park Güell.

beyond by a perimeter wall. Unfortunately, this grand vision turned out to be a utopia and never came to fruition. All that was actually built was a park and a small cluster of houses – but what a park!

Gaudí began to work his magic here in 1900. Back then this area was beyond the city, and the terrain was barren and rocky, without vegetation. The intention was to create a housing development and luxurious park inspired by the famous English garden city movement. Such developments were popular at the time because they offered a welcome contrast to the increasing industrialization of the expanding cities. Original plans foresaw sixty plots with forty homes, providing housing for around four hundred people – in those days, well-off families easily comprised

ten people, including children and servants. But in fact only three houses were built. One of them, Casa Muntaner, was occupied by the Güell family, one by the lawyer Trias, while Gaudí himself moved into another house. This pink stuccoed and richly decorated building in the middle of the park is now a museum and open to the public.

The bare, rocky terrain was difficult to cultivate. Rising to the challenge, Gaudí planted the area full of pine trees, palms and cacti and came up with an ingenious irrigation system. He was constantly inspired by the forms of nature, and in Park Güell he achieved a supreme balance between the manmade and the natural. One of the ways he did this was by using materials available on the site. With stones and rubble excavated from the hillside, Gaudí created promenades which look so natural you can scarcely believe they haven't always been here. The stone columns supporting the pathways are easily mistaken for the trunks of palm trees. Another great source of inspiration for the park was the classical Greek Sanctuary of Apollo at Delphi. Its influence can chiefly be seen in the space intended as a market hall, and the terrace above, which would have been the market place or public assembly area. The roof of the market hall is supported by Doric columns and forms the floor of the terrace.

Details from Gaudí's former home in Park Güell. This is now a museum.

Approaching the terrace from the park's main entrance, halfway up the staircase, you pass a huge dragon covered in colourful mosaic tiles with water spurting from its mouth. This sculpture represents Python, guardian of the subterranean waters. That's because, behind him, hidden from view, lies a rainwater storage cistern with a capacity of 12,000 litres (3,200 gallons). This collection basin was intended to give the residents of the park a measure of independence and to supply the irrigation system. The terrace is perfectly level, yet even when there is heavy rainfall, the water flows away. The architect achieved this by using a semi-porous layer of stones and sand for the floor rather than concrete. The water seeps through the floor, is carried in numerous small pipes to the columns (which are in fact hollow) and is drained through them into the water cistern.

The central terrace is enclosed by a wavy, mosaic-covered, seemingly endless wall. This wall has a dual purpose: it keeps people both out and in (the drop beyond is precipitously steep), and it is also an enormous bench, whose serpentine twists and turns are a perfect place to relax, chat and enjoy the views over the city. Thousands of colourful pieces of tile and glass were used for the extravagant decoration of this structure, which was the responsibility of architect Josep Maria Jujol, then working as Gaudí's young assistant but later a renowned architect in his own right. And believe it or not, this stone bench is actually very comfortable to sit on. Gaudí ensured this by moulding its shape to that of an imprint created by a naked man sitting on the plaster when it was still soft. This wonderful bench invites you to flop down, pleasantly tired, and enjoy the atmosphere of this special place. Its sinuous curving form creates intimate sitting areas in an otherwise open space, making it a meeting place for young and old: for the elderly, for young lovers, for residents of the city, but definitely also for tourists. Following the death of Eusebi Güell in 1918 and the failure of the project as a real estate venture, the park was sold to the city authorities of Barcelona. It has been open to the public since 1923, and was designated a World Heritage Site in 1984.

Above and opposite: **Details from the large wall and adjoining bench in the 'market place'. Despite the hard materials, the bench is comfortable and inviting.** Following pages: **A dragon fountain representing Python, guardian of the subterranean waters.**

Antoni Gaudí has not only left Barcelona with sparkling architectural masterpieces, but, in Park Güell, has provided a dynamic and dazzling city with an oasis of calm. Just as cruising across the open sea is the spirit-soothing antidote to the busy bustle of port life, so Park Güell will restore your sense of peace and equilibrium after a few hours spent exploring this exciting city.

Miami
See and be seen

Miami is the southernmost big city in the United States, and one of the main ports of call for cruise ships in the world. Every year, countless holidaymakers set off from here on a cruise to the Caribbean. You shouldn't miss the chance to take a tour of the city and of Miami Beach, whether before, after or during a cruise.

The story of Miami Beach is inextricably bound up with the name of Carl Fisher. More than just a strip of sand, Miami Beach is in fact a long narrow island covering 14 square kilometres (3,500 acres) just off the coast of mainland Miami. At the beginning of the 20th century, Fisher reinvented this island as a classic holiday destination, draining its marshy land, doubling it in size, and transforming it into a tropical paradise of beaches and palm trees. He also gave it the name Miami Beach. In the emerging age of the motorcar, Fisher was a

Miami Beach: by the 1970s, there was not much of it left.

A typical Art Deco building. Opposite above: **Miami beach life is very much an extension of the city.** Opposite below: **Lifeguards keep watch from brightly coloured wooden pavilions.**

pioneering force behind the 'Dixie Highway', which by the early 1920s extended from Ontario, Canada, all the way across the United States to the southern tip of the Florida Peninsula. He also financed the construction of the longest wooden bridge in the world to connect Miami Beach to the mainland; until then, a ferry was the only way across. He built hotels and casinos, and successfully brought his new holiday paradise to the attention of the whole of the United States by means of an ingenious publicity campaign: in 1921, he allowed his baby elephant Rosie to pose as a golf caddy for holidaymakers, who happened to include president elect Warren Harding. The photo was printed in newspapers nationwide. Billboard posters of scantily clad bathing beauties enjoying the white beaches and blue ocean waters also appeared around the country. A neon advertisement in Times Square announced 'It's June in Miami' – there were great holidays to be had in Florida even when it was cold in New York.

It has had its ups and downs, but Miami Beach today is more popular than ever as a holiday destination. The modern city has a cosmopolitan atmosphere thanks to its many Latin American residents, mainly Cuban refugees. The city is also popular for its balmy climate, partying lifestyle, the deep blue water of Biscayne Bay, and of course the wide sandy beaches. That wasn't the case in the 1970s, however. Building activity and coastal erosion had led to the virtual disappearance of the beach – not good for a city promoting itself as a tourist destination. So the national US Army Corps of Engineers was called in to help restore the beach with millions of tons of sand. Only when the width reached 90 metres (300 feet) and a cost of around 50 million dollars was the city administration satisfied. The beach stretches from Sunny Isles in the north to South Point Park in the south and is 16 kilometres (10 miles) long. It is made up of numerous different segments, each with their own character and crowd. Colourful wooden shelters dot the sand, from where well-built lifeguards keep a reassuring eye on everything.

As well as the beach proper, Miami Beach also has a significant cultural

In 1921, Miami entrepreneur Carl Fisher allowed his baby elephant Rosie to pose as a golf caddy for holidaymakers.

attraction: the 20th-century Art Deco District is a unique area boasting the largest collection of Art Deco architecture in the world. There are around eight hundred buildings in just 2.5 square kilometres (one square mile). Most of these buildings date from the 1930s and 1940s, when their style was known as Moderne (the term Art Deco, an abbreviation of the French 'Arts Décoratifs', was applied to this movement retrospectively in the 1960s). This style was an optimistic celebration of modernity and the machine age. It was characterized by geometric patterning, strong horizontals, clean curves and lines. In Florida many Art Deco buildings were given an added tropical flavour, with decoration featuring palm trees and flamingoes. Others have nautical detailing, such as railings and porthole windows, inspired by the magnificent cruise liners of the period, which themselves were among the finest expressions of Art Deco design.

The building boom of the interwar years was closely related to the emergence of mass tourism. Unfortunately, along with tourism Miami also attracted drugs, gamblers and notoriety (Al Capone died here in 1947). The city acquired a dubious reputation and over the years many of its historic Art Deco treasures fell into disrepair and were converted into low-rent retirement apartments.

Fortunately, in the 1980s, a renaissance was launched, spearheaded by the fashion business as modelling agencies moved in and the city became one of the most popular backdrops to fashion photoshoots in the world. Extensive renovations in the Art Deco District gradually restored the area to its former glory. During the course of this restoration, the colours were changed: instead of modest shades, a palette of cheerful pastel colours was introduced. Although historically speaking not strictly accurate, this gave the buildings a real charisma and emphasizes their marvellous original surface decorations.

The finest examples of Miami's elegant Art Deco buildings are the hotels on Ocean Drive, also the main street for restaurants and nightclubs. For those who like people-watching, this is a perfect

Opposite: **Art Deco buildings often have neon signs in the same style.** Below: **Rounded corners are one of the characteristic features of Art Deco architecture.**

spot to hang out in the evenings. Miami Beach is hip and not afraid to show it. Expensive cars drive by the outdoor cafés with their windows down, pumping music out at top volume. See and be seen is more than just a motto, it's a way of life here. The Art Deco District is now the most chic area in the whole of Miami and Miami Beach put together. It is often referred to as 'America's Riviera'. The place is even livelier today than it was in the bustling 1930s. There are many organized activities such as special Art Deco weekends and guided tours, but you can just as easily go exploring by yourself, making regular stops in the area's inviting outdoor cafés to sit and watch the world go by. America's Riviera is still as fascinating as ever.

Right: **The sleek lines of an Art Deco building.** Opposite: **Lots of fresh pastel colours were used when these buildings were renovated in the 1980s.**

Glittering city of Tsars

Some three hundred years ago, Tsar Peter the Great decided that Russia needed a northerly port offering access to the Baltic Sea and opening Russia up to trade with the West.

Sphinxes give an exotic touch to this city built by Peter the Great.
Opposite: **Domes of the Naval Cathedral of St Nicholas of the Sea.**

The city Peter planned to build alongside that port was to be in the style of a Western metropolis. The intention from the outset was that in beauty it should be the equal of the most splendid cities of Europe. Peter the Great was successful in his aim: St Petersburg is still a breathtakingly beautiful, European-style city. However, the creation of this urban jewel certainly took some doing. Sweden, then one of the most powerful countries in Europe, felt threatened by the project and declared war on Russia. But this did not hold Peter back, and in May 1703 he began building a dockyard and the Peter and Paul Fortress, after which the city on the River Neva was called.

Although Amsterdam, the city which he took as his example, was built predominantly in wood, the tsar decided that St Petersburg must be built of stone. This was no easy task on marshland where there was no stone available locally. The sheer scale of the building work created a national shortage of stone, leading to a ban on the construction of masonry buildings elsewhere in Russia.

The building of the city progressed with difficulty. Working conditions were so terrible that around 40,000 peasants, criminals and Swedish prisoners of war who had been set to work perished. St Petersburg became known as the 'city built on bones'. Peter subsequently set to work on a system of dykes inspired by those of Holland in order to drain the marshy land between the various rivers and ditches, though the area remains prone to flooding to this day. Thousands of Russians from other parts of the country received orders to pack their possessions and move to this unpopular, drizzly region where food prices were three times what they were in Moscow. It may have been heavy-handed, but it was

ruthlessly effective. In 1712, barely nine years after the foundation stones were laid, St Petersburg was declared the new capital of Russia and the government moved there from Moscow. When the tsar died in 1725, his new city had a population of 40,000.

Today there are around four million people living in St Petersburg; it is the second-largest city in Russia. The main landmarks and tourist attractions are on Fontanka, one of forty-two islands that make up the city. Fontanka is easily recognized from afar from the towering gold-coloured dome of St Isaac's Cathedral, built in the 19th century. It is the perfect landmark. Its beauty and that of many other buildings on the island is thanks to Peter the Great's successors. Tsarina Elizabeth was particularly unrestrained, giving her baroque Italian chief architect

The Trinity Cathedral towers over the city.

The extravagant Catherine the Great procured more than 2,500 paintings, 10,000 sculptures and 10,000 drawings with which to adorn her palaces.

Bartolomeo Rastrelli free rein. His masterpiece is the Winter Palace, which stands on the banks of the Neva.

The Winter Palace is spectacular, both inside and out. Its exterior is lavishly adorned with columns, gold leaf and a skyline studded with statuary. The interior is majestic, with famous features including the Jordan Staircase, the Small

Throne Room and the Malachite Room (for which more than two tons of ornamental stone were used, alongside gilded doors and a gilded ceiling). Even if there were no works of art hanging in the museum, the beauty of the building is undeniable; however, the masterpieces displayed here provide the climax to any visit. The Winter Palace is one of a group of buildings that together

Above: **Sometimes you come across relics from the Communist period.** Below: **A ship on the banks of the Neva.** Following pages: **The Winter Palace, now part of the Hermitage Museum.**

The Church of the Saviour of the Spilt Blood.

house the Hermitage Museum. The art collection amassed by the extravagant Catherine II – known as Catherine the Great – between 1764 and 1774 is vast. As well as a great deal of silver and porcelain, she procured more than 2,500 paintings, 10,000 sculptures and 10,000 drawings with which to adorn her palaces. Today, this collection forms the heart of the Hermitage, following the acquisition by the state of all imperial property after the Revolution in 1917. There are works by old masters Leonardo da Vinci, Michelangelo, Caravaggio and El Greco, and the collection of Rembrandts is legendary; there is also a fascinating collection of 20th-century art, including several works by Matisse and Gauguin.

There is in fact far too much art to take in in one day. The same goes for St Petersburg itself: you are unlikely to tire of this Venice of the North. Culture vultures will enjoy the magnificent baroque cathedral of SS Peter and Paul, the Russian Museum, the Naval Cathedral of St Nicholas of the Sea and the Mariinsky Theatre (a theatre visit is a must). When your appetite for culture is exhausted, a delightful activity is simply to stroll along the city's main shopping street, Nevsky Prospekt, where you will find French and Italian designer boutiques alongside authentic Russian department stores.

St Petersburg is an ideal city to visit by ship. Most cruise companies choose – quite rightly – to spend

Above: **Even in May, it can still be extremely cold.** Left: **A passageway from the museum square to Nevsky Prospekt; A postbox; A detail from the Church of the Saviour of the Spilt Blood built on the site of Alexander II's assassination.**

A statue covered in snow. Right: The Trinity Cathedral. Opposite: The freestanding clock tower of the Naval Cathedral of St Nicholas of the Sea.

several days here. In view of the harsh winter weather, most cruises take place between May and September (although there can still be snow in May). Because of its northerly latitude, the sun only goes down between 2 a.m. and 3 a.m. from mid-June to mid-July, and it is never completely dark. All kinds of musical festivities take place during these so-called 'white nights'. The streets are full of revellers, and young people dance and party all night long in the squares and parks. During the summer months when the River Neva is not

frozen, the bridges are opened up at night to allow ships to pass along – be sure to check the schedules and not to get stranded on the wrong side or you may be there until morning.

Several Russian companies and a few Western ones too run cruises between Moscow and St Petersburg, present and former capitals of Russia. So the old city of tsars is the ideal starting point for a journey of discovery into modern-day Russia.

6

River cruises

A river cruise is a distinctly different experience from a cruise at sea. For a start there is always something to see during the journey, since land is always in sight (it is true that on sea cruises the view can become a little monotonous). The better river cruise ships have a large terrace on the top deck with comfortable wooden deckchairs, from where you can enjoy this ever-changing scenery. The ships are naturally much smaller and more intimate than most seagoing cruise ships, making it easier to find your way around and to get to know your fellow passengers. There is less entertainment – no casinos, full-size theatres or cinemas; no multitude of bars and restaurants – although modern river cruise ships do generally have a restaurant, lounge, shop and sometimes a swimming pool (sometimes even a heated indoor pool). A river cruise is also a good option for people who enjoy sailing but are afraid of becoming seasick. Although modern stabilizers mean this is seldom a problem on today's seagoing cruise ships, a rolling wave motion is still a constant on the open sea.

There are river cruises on every continent: in Europe you can sail down the Rhine, the Danube, the Elbe or the Po. Since the opening of the Main–Danube Canal in 1992, it has been possible to cruise all the way from the North Sea to the Black Sea. In Africa, the Nile is an ideal route for exploring the ancient temples and treasures of Egypt; while in Russia, holidaymakers favour the Volga, the Don and the Neva. In the United States, attractive paddle steamers sail the Mississippi. Australia's most famous river route is the Murray, whose lush banks are an oasis of unique outback wildlife. In South America, you can cruise through rainforest along the Amazon and the Orinoco and even try your hand at piranha fishing. In China, more than sixty cruise ships sail past the towering gorges and ancient cities along the Yangtze. The length of a cruise can vary from a few days to a week

Opposite: **Feluccas on the Nile. A trip on these traditional fishing boats is a popular day excursion during a Nile cruise.**

or longer. All river cruises visit a variety of different ports of call, primarily during the day, and it is possible to book organized excursions. The on-board atmosphere tends to be relaxed rather than formal. Bear in mind that Egyptian or Chinese ships are usually less luxurious than those operated by American or European companies, despite their often impressive array of stars (in Egypt in particular, cruise companies can be excessively liberal with their star allocations). Nevertheless, most ships offering river cruises have air-conditioning, cabins with private bathrooms, and a sundeck from which to enjoy the view.

During my Nile cruise I had a cabin with a balcony, which I would thoroughly recommend: the ever-changing landscape passes by like a film.

Opposite and below: **Cruising on the distinctive yellow waters of the Yangtze.**

As always, it's a question of taste, but a river cruise can often be even more relaxing than a sea cruise, where the number of activities on offer is frequently so great that just reading the daily programme can raise the blood pressure. There is just so much going on! A more limited range of activities makes life so much simpler. But that doesn't mean a river cruise need be dull – far from it. You simply have more time and peace and quiet in the evening to digest all the impressions and new experiences of each day.

The Nile # A voyage through
history

The Nile was the great life-giving artery of ancient Egypt, whose

magnificent temples and monuments still cluster on the river's banks.

Today there is no better way to explore them than by cruise.

At nearly **7,000** kilometres (4,350 miles), the Nile is not only the longest river in Africa, but in the world. It has its source in Lake Victoria, where it begins life as the White Nile. Further north, near Khartoum in Sudan, it is joined and strengthened by the short but powerful Blue Nile, which flows into the White Nile's clearer waters. In Egypt, the Nile flows north from Lake Nasser until it splits at Cairo into multiple branches that feed the fertile Nile Delta between Rashid and Port Said, an area of around 23,000 square kilometres (9,000 square miles).

The Nile is Egypt's lifeline. In the 5th century BC, Herodotus wrote that Egypt was 'a gift from the Nile'. Or, as the local population says, 'Egypt is the Nile and the Nile is Egypt'. The banks of the river are as green an oasis today as they were centuries ago in the time of the pharaohs, when the river would annually burst its banks and bring fertile silt to the land. Even from the top deck of a cruise ship you can clearly see the difference between the verdant green strip that borders the river and the dry yellow sands of the desert beyond, stretching as far as the eye can see. Around 70 per cent of Egypt is made up of this arid terrain. The river is also a major thoroughfare and an abundant source of fish and tourist income.

The ancient Egyptians believed that Hapi, the god of the Nile's annual inundation, was responsible for

Opposite: **Statue of Ramses II at Karnak.**
Below: **Chephren's Sphinx and the Pyramid of Cheops.**
Previous pages: **Aswan Lake.**

the prosperity of the population. This god, who was depicted as a man with a beard and women's breasts (a symbol of fertility), had a bottomless urn from which water flowed. The people believed that he lived in a cave in the Aswan hills that was guarded by snakes, and hoped to win his favour by making plentiful offerings. For if he held his urn at a slant, Hapi would bring about the all-important annual flooding of the Nile. Too slanting and it would result in a deluge; not slanting enough meant drought and therefore famine.

The flooding was in reality caused by summer rains and snowmelt in the Ethiopian Highlands, which swelled the rivers at the Nile's source and caused flooding all along its course. This happened every year for millennia until 1971, when the Aswan Dam was completed. Controlled irrigation is now possible the whole year round and the annual inundation no longer occurs. There are disadvantages, however, one being that the river's rich silt, so useful to Egyptian agriculture in the past, is no longer deposited. Fertility has declined in some places as a result, and the desert is clearly encroaching on once verdant land. The current of the Nile is also much weaker.

It is no surprise that the ancient pharaohs built temples on the banks of this river that was so central to their

A Nile cruise is the most ideal way to reach a vast array of unforgettable treasures.

Left: **A felucca on the Nile.** Right: **An obelisk rises proudly into the sky.** Below: **Images of the enormous temple complex at Karnak.**

Previous pages: **Part of the Great Hypostyle Hall at Karnak. Some of the columns are 24 metres (78 feet) high.**

civilization and their power. Ramses II, who ruled Egypt for 67 years from 1279 until 1212 BC, left a particularly impressive legacy. Of all the temples still preserved in Egypt, around half were built under his rule. One of the highlights is the enormous temple complex of Karnak in Luxor, one of the oldest tourist attractions in the world. In its day, Luxor – or Thebes as it was known in ancient times – was one of the biggest cities in the world. At the time of Napoleon's campaigns in 1798, Luxor became the latest thing. In the wake of the emperor, an army of scholars, archaeologists and artists began investigating the relics of the impressive ancient Egyptian civilization. Everything was carefully documented and recorded, feeding and fuelling a huge appetite for all things Egyptian in Europe. The enormous temple city of Luxor contains some of the most important monuments from ancient Egypt. Pharaoh after pharaoh enlarged the city by erecting bigger and bigger buildings, each determined to outdo his predecessors. The Great Hypostyle Hall of Ramses II is particularly awe-inspiring: a forest of 134 giant carved columns, some of them over 24 metres (78 feet) high. It is spectacular and humbling to walk among them. Just thinking what a task it must have been to build this with the technologies available at the time – the 13th century BC – one can feel nothing but respect.

Across the Nile from Luxor lies the Valley of the Kings, the burial place of Egyptian rulers for hundreds of years. The most famous of these is undoubtedly that of the boy pharaoh Tutankhamen. The discovery of his tomb by Howard Carter in 1922 was one of the biggest archaeological sensations of the last

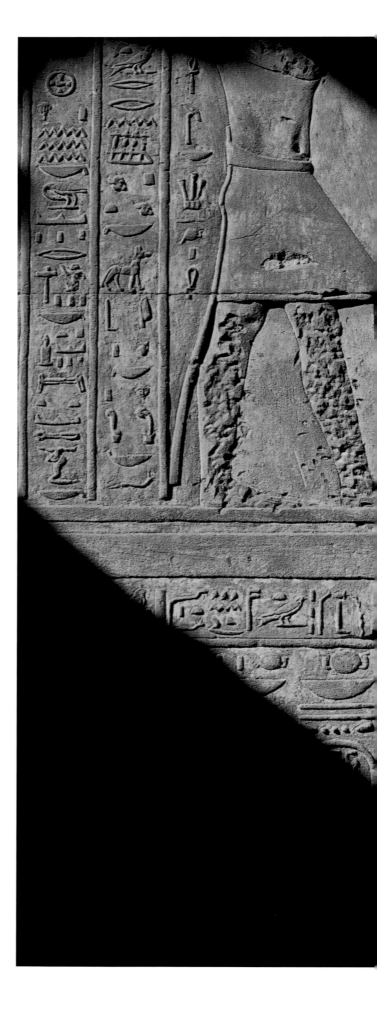

Sunlight and shadows on a panel of ancient hieroglyphs.
Following pages: **The Step Pyramid of King Djoser in Saqqara, built around 3000 bc.**

century. Although it had been partially robbed in ancient times, most of the tomb's funerary equipment was found in excellent condition, and included the sarcophagus and mummified body of Tutankhamen himself, bearing his famous gold mask. However, visitors today should be aware that the tomb is not so spectacular as many others in the valley, and its treasures are now in the Cairo Museum. If time is limited, you won't be missing too much if you choose not to come here.

Most cruises go between Luxor and Aswan, which takes four days. There is also the option to sail between Cairo and Aswan over twelve to fifteen days. Around three hundred cruise ships sail along the Nile during the Egyptian winter; far fewer in the baking hot summer. Don't expect too much luxury, however many stars a cruise company may claim for its vessels. But most do have English-speaking guides on board, and in any case, a Nile cruise is about the destinations and not the ship. It is quite simply the most ideal way to reach a vast array of unforgettable cultural treasures.

Sailing past castles and windmills

The Rhine begins its journey high in the mountains of Switzerland. As it makes its way northwards it passes through numerous historic cities, before dividing into multiple branches in the Netherlands and finally emptying into the North Sea. The river is one of Europe's most popular cruise routes.

As it streams its way along a length of 1,320 kilometres (820 miles) the Rhine crosses or borders six countries – Switzerland, Liechtenstein, Austria, Germany, France and the Netherlands. It is one of the longest and most important rivers in Europe. Yet it does not flow out to sea under its own name; once it reaches the Netherlands it splits off into numerous different branches including the Waal, the IJssel, the Old Rhine and the Lek. Rotterdam, the biggest port in Europe (and, after Shanghai, the biggest in the world), is on the banks of one of these smaller rivers, the Nieuwe Maas, and so is connected to the Rhine. It is no surprise, therefore, that a great deal of freight is carried along the river. Fortunately, there is still plenty of space on the water for cruise ships. A wide variety of companies offer cruises following many different routes. Indeed holidaymakers can cruise all the way from Amsterdam to Budapest, the North Sea to the Black Sea, something that was impossible before the 1992 opening of the Main–Danube Canal.

Rheinstein Castle is one of many that stand along the banks of the Rhine.

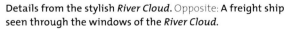

Details from the stylish *River Cloud*. Opposite: **A freight ship seen through the windows of the *River Cloud*.**

The Main is a tributary of the Rhine, and linking the two great rivers, the Rhine and the Danube, created a much greater variety of sailing routes and gave a considerable boost to the popularity of river cruises.

If the connection of the Rhine to the Danube was a dream come true for cruise companies, it was a scheme first dreamed of many centuries earlier by

the Frankish King Charlemagne. In the 8th century AD he set thousands of labourers to work digging a canal, the Fossa Carolina, between the rivers Rezat and Altmühl. But as his biographer Einhard reported, he had to abandon his efforts because incessant rain and thunderstorms were thwarting the project: the ditch constantly filled with water and its banks collapsed. A section of the Fossa Carolina, called Karlsgraben, still exists, but Charlemagne's dream was not to be realized in his lifetime. It was not until many centuries later that King Ludwig I of Bavaria

Many historic cities lie on the Rhine.
A cruise is an ideal way to encounter
different European cultures.

Splendid castles such as Stahleck make popular day trip destinations. Opposite: **The lounge is a pleasant place to relax.**

picked up the project, this time with more success. The building of the Ludwig Canal, which followed more or less the same route as the modern canal, was completed in 1845. All kinds of vessels used this connection between the Main and the Danube for several decades before it fell into relative disuse, superseded by the railways, which took over a lot of goods transportation from shipping in the later 19th century. Construction began on the modern Main–Danube Canal in 1959. Running from Bamberg to Kelheim, it is 171 kilometres (106 miles) long – twice the length of the Panama Canal – and took thirty years of intensive work to build.

Most Rhine cruises last a week. They are becoming ever more popular among Europeans, who now account for more than half of passengers, although Americans

Although the *River Cloud* looks as though she was built in the 1930s, she only came into service in 1996. Warm shades of wood and lots of brass contribute to her elegant style.

are still the majority. In these days of constantly increasing road traffic congestion, it makes sense that cruises have overtaken coach travel in popularity. Since so many historic cities lie on the Rhine, a cruise is an ideal way to encounter different European cultures, as well as to explore the magnificent castles that stand proud on the clifftops along the river's route. From these strongholds, powerful medieval overlords surveyed their terrain and levied tolls on the passing merchant traffic. Cruise ships are moored in the evening, giving you plenty of opportunity to discover the nightlife of the various ports of call. A city centre is never very far away, often within walking distance.

The *River Cloud* is one of the ships that regularly cruises along not just the Rhine, but also the Moselle, the Main and the Danube, as well as Dutch rivers and

lakes (after all, 20 per cent of the Netherlands is made up of water). Built in the style of the 1930s with lots of wood and brass, this ship has all the comfort and facilities one would expect on an ultra-luxurious river cruise. For despite her authentic period character, the *River Cloud* in fact only came into service in 1996. She has a fine restaurant, as well as a library, boutique, beauty salon, sauna and fitness room. An elegant lounge complete with Steinway grand piano is the setting for classical concerts and frequent lectures about the places visited en route.

Today, the River Cloud *is leaving the country of windmills and tulips and travelling upstream along the Rhine from Arnhem into Germany. There is a lot of fascinating activity on the water, predominantly freight transportation. And there are magnificent far-reaching views. The flat, watery Dutch polder landscape, so much of it reclaimed from the sea, gradually solidifies into the hilly and forested lands of Germany, where splendid castles surrounded by trees wait to be visited.*

What can be better than to relax on the teak deck of
the River Cloud and enjoy the ever-changing scenery?
At least, for the time being. Because the weather looks
as if it is about to turn: the sun has disappeared
behind the clouds and a breeze is developing.
The clouds are growing steadily greyer and more
menacing. The weather forecast is not good; there is
a storm brewing. In this region, and at this time of
year, they can be very severe. My thoughts drift back to
Charlemagne and his heroic failure to link the Rhine
and the Danube. The first drops start to fall. Centuries

Windmills in the flat Netherlands landscape.
Opposite: Interior and exterior railings on the *River Cloud*.

may pass, but some things never change. I decide to
go down to the ship's lounge where I can continue to
sip my drink and enjoy a piano recital... At least some
things have changed for the better.

The Yangtze Towering rocks and harmonious gardens

The magnificent rock formations that flank the Yangtze, the longest river in Asia, have inspired poets and artists for millennia.

The spectacular landscape of the Three Gorges is a work of art by nature herself.

At the beginning of the evening, it was already dark. The Yangtze Pearl *dropped anchor unexpectedly. Not alongside a quay, but more or less right in the middle of the river. There was no opportunity to disembark. The captain decided upon this emergency measure because if the ship were to sail on, we would have missed one of the most beautiful gorges along the route. Our day's excursion overran its schedule, sailing up the river took longer than expected, and as a result we failed to reach the famous Qutang Gorge during daylight. This meant a 6 a.m. start this morning to make up time. But Captain Wang certainly knows his river: this gorge is sublime. True, the air is hazy with humidity, but that is a constant of the Yangtze landscape. Either side of us towering cliffs rise almost vertically out of the water. These rocks are real-life versions of the washed ink drawings that are sold everywhere on souvenir stalls. Some of them are over 1,000 metres (3,200 feet) high. At the top they look as if they are about to melt into the thin fog at any moment, giving them a mystical air that has inspired innumerable Chinese landscape artists.*

Opposite: **The Daning River, a branch of the Yangtze.** Top: A cruise ship sails through the impressive rock mass of Xiling Gorge.

Details of the ancient town of Fengdu, known to the Chinese as the 'Ghost City', whose numerous temples depict fantastic underworld demons and gods.

The Yangtze splits China in two horizontally. It starts in Qinghai province and runs from west to east before finally flowing into the Yellow Sea near Shanghai. The word Yangtze is a corruption of Chang Jiang, which means 'long river' in Yangzhou dialect. It is true to its name. At around 6,300 kilometres (3,900 miles), it is the third longest river in the world after the Nile and the Amazon. The most scenic section runs between Yichang and Chongqing, and naturally this is where most cruise ships sail. It is the location of the Three Gorges, where the river winds its way between vertical cliff faces created around seventy million years ago by a shift in the earth's crust. The 75-kilometre (46-mile) Xiling Gorge, the 45-kilometre (28-mile) Wu (or Witches) Gorge and the 8-kilometre (5-mile) Qutang Gorge are the highlights of a cruise along the Yangtze.

The Xiling Gorge is in fact made up of seven smaller gorges, each one named after the shape or colour of its rocks, with splendidly evocative results including Ox Liver, Horse Lung and Shadow Play Gorges. Other

rock formations have lyrical names, such as Military Book and Precious Sword Gorge. The Yangtze has a total of seven hundred tributaries or distributaries. In this area, tributaries such as the Daning, which flows into the Yangtze near Wushan, are still more impressive, if that is possible.

Just downstream from the Three Gorges lies the controversial Three Gorges Dam, the biggest hydro-engineering project in the world. Stretching more than 2 kilometres (1.25 miles) across the width of the Yangtze River, the dam feeds what is set to become the world's largest hydroelectric power station, capable of supplying around 10 per cent of Chinese households (130 million people) with electricity. The hope is that it will also control the periodic flooding of the Yangtze Valley, which has caused death and devastation time and again through China's history. In 1931, the death toll from drowning, disease and starvation was 145,000, and almost as many died just four years later in 1935.

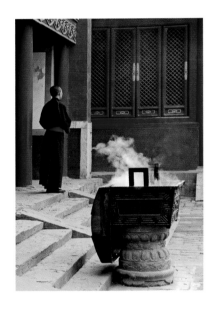

Travel, and you will meet a wide variety of different people. Opposite: **A Chinese woman daydreams on the banks of the Yangtze.**

However, the environmental and human impact of the Three Gorges Dam project is vast. As the waters rise at a rapid rate in the reservoir behind the dam, unique scenic areas as well as archaeological and cultural sites are disappearing for ever. This reservoir will eventually be some 600 kilometres (375 miles) in length. There are also grave concerns that pollution will accumulate behind the dam, as much of the waste from big cities upstream is channelled straight into the Yangtze. Worldwide protests have been of no avail. The project was begun in 1992 and is scheduled to be completed in 2009, although an overrun of a few years can be expected, not least because some one hundred and forty towns situated on the banks have to be evacuated and demolished. Around 1.3 million people are in the process of being relocated to new towns and villages built at a higher level. Many historic buildings are being dismantled and rebuilt. The water in the reservoir will ultimately be 175 metres (575 feet) above sea level, and the scenery of the Three Gorges themselves will change considerably as the river rises and widens.

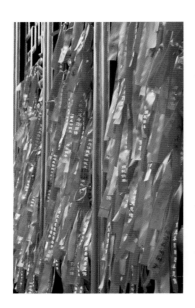

Images of temples and gardens, oases of calm. Ponds containing ornamental fish are a common feature of Chinese gardens.

This is the new, rapidly modernizing China, and the banks of the Yangtze are no stranger to heavy industry. Smoking chimneys and polluted quays are frequent sights both before and after the Three Gorges. But they are in marked contrast to another, much more refined phenomenon. The Yangtze River area is home to numerous classical Chinese gardens, which count among the greatest examples of Chinese artistic expression. Historically, designing the ideal garden was an art form on a par with poetry and painting. There are more than one hundred and fifty preserved gardens in the region of the city of Suzhou. Founded in the 6th century BC, this elegant city was built with a complete network of canals designed to regulate the water level of the Yangtze when it burst its banks. In the centuries that followed, Suzhou became an important cultural centre, and rich citizens invested their money in the creation of fine gardens. The most beautiful examples are the Humble Administrator's Garden, which dates from the 9th century, and the Master of the Nets Garden, which dates from 1140.

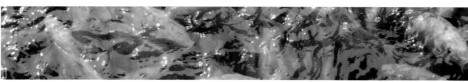

Above: **Detail from a garden pavilion.**
Right: **Footbridge to the temples in Fengdu.** Opposite: **Cruising through the Qutang Gorge.**

A classical Chinese garden represented nature in microcosm. Composed of the basic elements of water, rocks, plants and buildings, it was designed in accordance with the Taoist principles of harmony. Each sense was to be artfully stimulated: sight by the elegant combination of nature and man-made structures; smell by the scent of plants and flowers; hearing by the trickle of water; and touch by different surfaces and textures. In its artful, man-made harmonies, such a space is the opposite of the sublime natural scenery of the Yangtze's soaring gorges – yet both in their way offer a profound, almost spiritual experience.

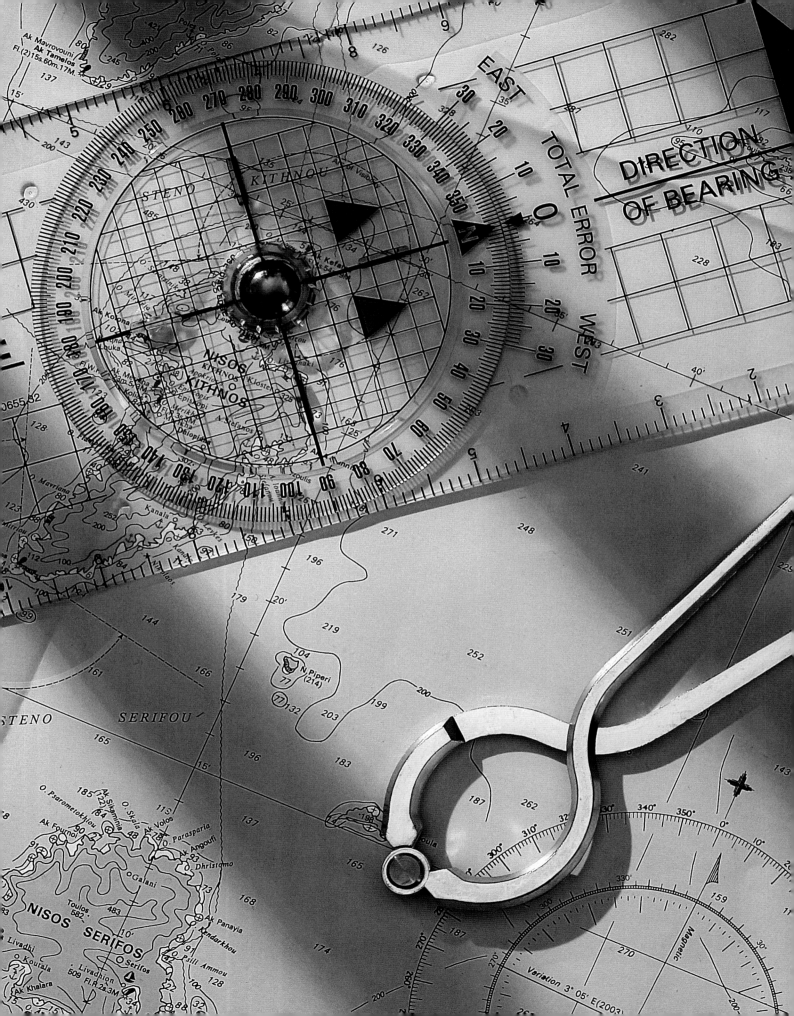

7

Legendary ships

1 pp 28–37 **Sea Cloud**

The four-masted **Sea Cloud** is 2,532 tons in size, has 34 cabins (all with a sea view) and can house a maximum of 69 passengers. The crew is made up of 60 people. Apart from lectures, there is not a great deal of entertainment: just an occasional performance by a pianist/singer, not to mention the crew, who perform as a sailors' chorus. The ship does not have a spa, swimming pool or fitness room. The **Sea Cloud** has a modern sister ship, the **Sea Cloud II**. This 3,849-ton ship came into service in 2001. It was built in a 1920s style, but the level of comfort is up-to-date, and this ship does have a fitness room and spa on board, including a sauna and steam room. As on the **Sea Cloud**, there are also facilities for water-skiing, wind-surfing and snorkelling. The 48 cabins with sea view can house a maximum of 96 guests, and the crew is 60-strong. Just like its sister ship, the three-masted barque is mainly suited to adults who enjoy sailing on a tall ship. Both ships are square-rigged and sail in different parts of the world – mainly the Caribbean and Europe – depending on the season. To find out where the ships are sailing, go to www.seacloud.com

1 pp 38–45 **Carnival**

It is always party time on Carnival ships. The fleet of the biggest cruise company in the world is undoubtedly impressive. The ships can be split into different classes. Holiday Class is made up of the (for Carnival, relatively small) **Celebration** (built in 1987, 1,486 passengers) and the **Holiday** (built in 1985, 1,452 passengers). Fantasy Class comprises the ships **Ecstasy, Elation, Fantasy, Fascination, Imagination, Inspiration, Paradise** and **Sensation**, all of which were built between 1990 and 1998 and can accommodate 2,052 passengers. The **Carnival Destiny** (1996), **Triumph** (1999) and **Victory** (2000) belong to the Destiny Class and have room for between 2,642 and 2,758 passengers. Shipbuilders must rejoice when they get a client like Carnival, whose Spirit Class vessels created work for thousands of people between 2001 and 2004. This class comprises the **Carnival Legend, Carnival Miracle, Carnival Pride** and **Carnival Spirit**, all of which are able to carry 2,124 guests. The latest class is called Conquest and is made up of the following ships: **Glory, Valor, Liberty, Freedom** and **Conquest**. They can accommodate 2,974 passengers. Two as yet unnamed ships are in the pipeline and will have room for 3,100 holidaymakers. Most of the ships sail in the Caribbean, but they also travel around Mexico, Alaska, Hawaii, New England and Canada, through the Panama Canal, and in the Mediterranean Sea. For more information, go to www.carnival.com

1 pp 46–55 **Queen Elizabeth 2**

The **Queen Elizabeth 2** measures 70,327 tons and has a capacity of 950 cabins for 1,728 passengers. Around 1,000 crew members keep the ship sailing. The dress code is predominantly formal. There are different organized activities each day, including high-quality lectures on a variety of subjects. There are five full-service formal restaurants and two informal restaurants. The ship has three classes (Grill, Caronia and Mauretania Class), and the restaurant(s) available to guests depend on the class they have chosen. Passengers travelling in the luxury Grill Class have the choice of the Queens Grill, Britannia Grill or Princess Grill. Passengers travelling Caronia class can dine in the restaurant of the same name, and guests from the lower-priced Mauretania Class dine in the Mauretania restaurant. There are male hosts to act as dance partners for ladies sailing alone, if required. The atmosphere on board is best described as cosmopolitan.

The **Queen Mary 2**, which is around twice as big (151,400 tons), goes that little bit further. It has two classes, Grill and Britannia Class, and four full-service restaurants. There are also a number of informal restaurants and snack opportunities. With 1,310 cabins (some 953 of which have a private balcony) for 2,620 passengers, this ship is more of a floating city, especially when one considers that there are also 1,253 crew members. With – among other facilities – three outdoor and two indoor pools, eight whirlpools, fourteen lounges and bars, a theatre, a state-of-the-art fitness room and spa, discos, a variety of boutiques and shops and a planetarium, it is unlikely that passengers will become bored. There are also special programmes for children. More information about both ships can be found at www.cunard.com.

Boutique options

There could not be a bigger contrast than that between ocean liners and boutique ships. Where ocean liners (and other modern cruise ships) are large and cater for the masses, with lots of entertainment on board, the small boutique ships – which can carry up to two hundred passengers – are intimate, with relatively little

entertainment on offer. No casinos, one-armed bandits, art auctions or extravagant theatre productions. On these ships, what matters is the peace and relaxation of sailing, the feeling of being on board your own yacht. On the top ships, both the food and service are of a very high standard indeed. There is no such word as 'no' as far as the crews are concerned. Alongside the **Sea Dream** *I* and *II* (both of which have space for 108 passengers, see www.seadreamyachtclub.com), the most luxurious segment of motor boutique ships includes the **Hebridean Princess** and **Hebridean Spirit** (with accommodation for 49 and 81 guests respectively, for more information go to www.hebridean.co.uk), and the Seabourn ships **Legend**, **Pride** and **Spirit** (all three of which can accommodate 200 guests, see www.seabourn.com).

In addition to this elite sector, there are also many other boutique ships offering a good service and surprising destinations, since small ships can reach places that other ships cannot. It is partly because of this that they provide passengers with an unequalled cruising experience, away from the masses.

Practical information
Legendary ships

Alternative cruises

2 pp 62–71 **Hurtigruten**

The modern Hurtigruten ships are extremely comfortable, although there can be noise during loading and unloading, including at night-time. Because Norway is so far north, there is a splendid period when the sun shines around the clock. This gives the journey a special atmosphere. The period during which night never falls varies according to location. In Honningsvåg, for example, this is from 13 May until 30 July, while in the more southerly Bodø, it is 3 June until 9 July. Conversely, there is also a period in winter when the sun does not appear on the horizon, and during this period the northern lights (aurora borealis) are regularly visible. In Honningsvåg, the sun is not seen between 18 November and 23 January, while the inhabitants of Bodø only go without sunlight between 15 and 28 December. More information is available at www.hurtigruten.com, where there are also precise travel details for the ships, for both the northern and southern routes.

2 pp 72–81 **Tall ships**

The tall ships operated by Star Clippers (the *Royal Clipper*, *Star Clipper* and *Star Flyer*), along with the *Sea Cloud* and the *Sea Cloud II* (see pages 28–37), offer a high level of luxury and comfort. Depending on the season, they sail in Europe, the Caribbean and Asia. More information can be found at www. star-clippers.com and www.seacloud. com. Alternatives include Windjammer Barefoot Cruises, which operates four smaller ships that accommodate between 64 and 122 passengers: the *Legacy*, the *Mandalay*, the *Polynesia* and the *Yankee Clipper*. More basic than the other tall ships, these only sail in the Caribbean and off the coast of Costa Rica. For more information, go to www.windjammer.com.

In a completely different category (because, in the eyes of sailors, these are not real sail ships) are the so-called sail cruise ships. These do have masts with sails, but the sails are hoisted at the touch of a button. There is no manpower involved. The engines are used often, especially when entering or leaving a port. These ships are the five-masted *Club Med 2* (349 passengers, see www.clubmed.com); the *Wind Surf*, another five-master with capacity for 308 passengers; and the smaller *Wind Spirit* and the *Wind Star*, both four-masters which can carry 148 passengers (www.windstarcruises. com).

2 pp 82–89 **Freight ships**

Cruising on freight ships is becoming increasingly popular. With space for a legal maximum of only twelve passengers per ship, the 250 or so that carry passengers (most owned by German shipping companies) are often fully-booked well in advance. It is therefore advisable to plan your trip well ahead. Do not forget to take out cancellation insurance, and it is also a good idea to take extra passport photos with you in case the ship calls in unexpectedly at a port where you need a visa. For most people, a regular freight ship will have more appeal than a containership, partly because they stay in port for longer. However, it is true that modern containerships – at least the bigger ones – are more stable in the water.

There are a variety of sites that can provide you with more information, including www.freighterworld.com, www.freightertravel.com, www. travel-tips.com, www.freightertrips. com and the New Zealand site www. freightertravel.co.nz.

Fascinating routes

3 pp 96–105 **Caribbean**

Anyone planning a cruise to the Caribbean can consider themselves lucky. This is the most popular cruise destination in the world, so the choice is enormous, from boutique ships and tall ships to mega-ships. All the big cruise companies sail here – Carnival in particular (www.carnival.com) is very active in the region – as well as innumerable smaller ones. From September to November is 'hurricane season', but this is of course taken into account by the cruise ships and it is very rare for a ship to get into danger, although occasionally the weather makes some ports difficult to reach and a route has to be changed.

Most cruises in this area are round trips, ending in the port where they began. The length of a cruise can vary from two to fourteen days, but most last a week. In addition to Miami and San Juan, popular points of departure include Florida's Fort Lauderdale, Tampa and Port Canaveral, not forgetting Barbados and even New York. Cruises to the eastern Caribbean tend to visit islands such as St Thomas, Puerto Rico, St Maarten, Dominica and Martinique; the western Caribbean

has ports of call like Jamaica, Cozumel (Mexico), the Cayman Islands and Belize. Some of these cruises even sail through the Panama Canal.

Many ships alternate an easterly with a westerly route, so anyone with two weeks on their hands can choose to follow the two routes consecutively without having to change ship. Cruises through the southern Caribbean will pass islands such as Aruba, Barbados, Curaçao, Antigua and Guadeloupe. For a quieter holiday, consider going between mid-April and mid-December, when these islands are less busy.

3 pp 106–113 **World cruises**

Where the choice of ships that sail in the Caribbean is large, the choice of ships offering world cruises is small. One reason is that these ships have to meet many more safety and technical requirements, as they are more likely to encounter adverse weather conditions en route. Again, the internet is a good source of advice, as are travel agents of course. The **Seven Seas Voyager** (www.rssc.com), the **Queen Elizabeth 2** (www.cunard.com) and the **Crystal Serenity** (www.crystalcruises.com) are a few of the ships that have completed round-the-world cruises. The **Saga Rose** and the **Saga Ruby** (www.saga.co.uk),

Practical information

Alternative cruises

Fascinating routes

both owned by the same company, have a tradition of both setting off on a world cruise from Southampton in the UK at the same time, the *Rose* sailing a westerly route and the *Ruby* an easterly one. Information about renting or buying an apartment on board the ship *The World* can be found at www.aboardtheworld.com.

3 pp 114–123 **French Polynesia**

Anyone wanting to go on a cruise in French Polynesia will first have to fly to Papeete, the capital of Tahiti, where the international airport is based. There are daily flights here from Los Angeles. The *Paul Gauguin* (www.rssc.com) is probably the most famous cruise ship that sails around the Society Islands the whole year round. This luxurious vessel, owned by Regent Seven Seas Cruises, is strikingly spacious, and can carry 320 passengers. There is room for more, but French law forbids it, and consequently the atmosphere on board is notably peaceful. The *Paul Gauguin* has a retractable platform at the rear, allowing guests to indulge in a variety of water sports, including water-skiing, snorkelling, windsurfing and diving.For those who would prefer to take a cruise in a small ship, Bora Bora Cruises (www.boraboracruises.com) is a good choice. The 70-metre

(230-foot) sister ships *Tia Moana* and *Tu Moana* each have 37 luxury cabins on board. A cruise lasts for seven days (six nights) and leaves Bora Bora to visit the islands of Taha'a, Raiatea and Huahine before returning to the point of departure. Their modest size means they can sail around the lagoons with ease. Completely different again are the freight ship cruises available in French Polynesia. You can choose from the *Aranui 2* or the more modern *Aranui 3*, among others. The latter does not impose an age limit, unlike most freight ships offering cruising possibilities. More information can be found at www.freighterworld.com or www.aranui.com.

Nature and expedition cruises

4 pp 130–141 **Antarctica**

The originator of cruises to Antarctica was the Swedish-born American Lars-Eric Lindblad, who organized the first cruise to the white continent in 1966. In 1969, he ordered the construction of the expedition ship *Lindblad Explorer*, which was to undertake regular cruises. It carried a hundred passengers on its maiden voyage. The *Lindblad Explorer* was later renamed *Society Explorer*, then just

Explorer. Today there are around thirty ships that sail to the southernmost continent between November and March. Nearly all cruises to Antarctica leave from Ushuaia in Argentina or Punta Arenas in Chile, before sailing through Drake Passage, which is notorious for its rough weather conditions. The traditional route goes to the Antarctic Peninsula; there is only one ship that goes further. There are a number of different types of ship that sail here. Small vessels such as the *Antarctic Dream* (www.antarctic.cl) can carry a maximum of 87 passengers and have a strengthened bow to help deal with the icy waters. The website www.victory-cruises.com lists small ships, including sail ships, that offer trips to Antarctica. Medium-sized ships that carry up to 300 people include the *Bremen* (164 passengers) and the *Hanseatic* (184 passengers; for both ships see www.hlkf.com). Large ships, which can transport one thousand people or more (such as *HAL*, *Crystal* and *Princess*), offer sightseeing tours only. There are no landings because of the large numbers of people. Advantages of travelling on a larger ship are that the costs of the cruise are lower and the on-board stabilizers are more effective. Finally there are the icebreakers such as the *Professor*

Multanovskiy (www.quark-expeditions.com), a relatively basic ship that carries just 49 passengers but, because of its shallow draft, can reach places that other cruise ships can only dream about.

4 pp 142–147 **Galapagos Islands**

The Galapagos Islands are 1,000 kilometres (620 miles) west of Ecuador. Every day there are several evening flights from Quito in Ecuador to Baltra or San Cristóbal on the Galapagos Islands. The luxurious and modern ship *Celebrity Xpedition* (www.celebritycruises.com) sails in Galapagos Island waters the whole year round. It has 47 cabins (including nine suites) and can accommodate a maximum of 92 passengers. Excursions are carried out under the supervision of Ecuadorian guides, and landings are made in Zodiacs (inflatable rubber boats). Many small ships sail in the area too, from basic converted fishing boats to high-end diving yachts. Some can only accommodate around ten guests. Information about local shipping companies and cruise ships can be found at www.galapagostraveller.com or www.galapagosislands.com. The period from December to May is the warm season, when the sea water is pleasant enough for snorkelling but there is also the chance of clouds and tropical rainstorms due to the high humidity. Even in the dry season (from June to December) there can be the occasional downpour, despite the characteristic blue sky. The diving is very good in this area, but bear in mind that the water currents can be relatively cold. A warm wetsuit is advisable.

4 pp 148–157 **South Patagonia**

There is a variety of cruising opportunities in South Patagonia, through both Argentinian and Chilean waters. The average length of a cruise varies from three to eight days. Cruceros Australis is a well-known shipping company which, with its two modern ships the *Mare Australis* (built 2002; 63 cabins) and the *Via Australis* (built 2006; 64 cabins), offers cruises through Patagonia to Tierra del Fuego and Cape Horn. This four- or five-day trip goes from Punta Arenas in Chile to Ushuaia in Argentina, or the other way round. There are expert lectures on the wildlife, geography and history of the region; these are available both on board and on land.

More information can be found at www.australis.com. The expedition ship the *Antarctic Dream* (39 cabins for

Practical information
Nature and expedition cruises

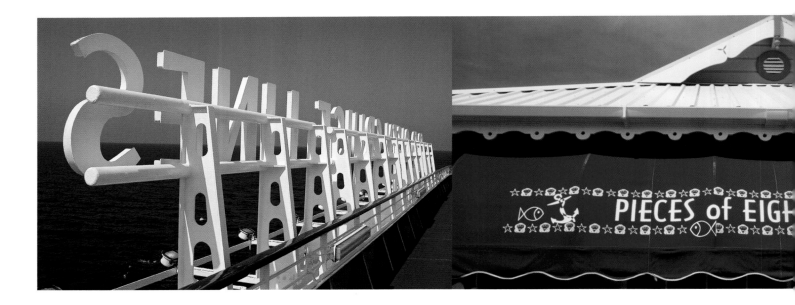

87 passengers; see www.antarctic.cl) does not only undertake cruises to the frozen continent from which it takes its name, but also four- and eight-day trips through the fjords of South Patagonia. The point of departure is Punta Arenas, and Ushuaia and Cape Horn are among its destinations. The programme features a helicopter flight over the D'Agostini Glacier, weather permitting. The trip is supervised by professional expedition leaders, who also give lectures on board.

Other ships that sail in this area can be found at www.chile-travel.com/chile-cruises.html and www.victory-cruises.com. Some large luxury ships, such as the **Golden Princess** (capacity 2,600 passengers), make trips to South Patagonia (see www.princess.com). With its enormous size and draft, the **Golden Princess** cannot access small fjords, but it can sail through the Strait of Magellan. It also takes a 'scenic route' around Cape Horn. The point of departure is Buenos Aires in Argentina, and the trip ends in Valparaíso (near Santiago) in Chile; or you can opt to make the journey in reverse. There are no opportunities to disembark.

Interesting ports of call

5 pp 164–173 **Barcelona**

In a city like Barcelona there is always something to do. At www.barcelona.com you will find useful up-to-date tips, including a city guide with listings of shops, restaurants, bars and clubs. There are also descriptions of a few key monuments by Gaudí that you should visit. In addition to the Sagrada Família, the cathedral that he began building in 1882 and is still unfinished, there is the famous Casa Milà, whose roof alone is worth a visit, if only for a sight of Gaudí's eccentrically shaped chimneys. As well as the Manzana de la Discordia, one can also visit the house that Gaudí built for his patron, Eusebi Güell. Palau Güell (Güell Palace) dates from 1888. The family has lived there for years. The best place to relax and gather one's thoughts is of course Park Güell, where the architect's former home has been transformed into a museum. There is also a club for Gaudí fans. If you go to www.gaudiclub.com, there is a lot of information available about the architect. The club organizes coach tours lasting a whole or half a day around the architectural high points in the city created by the master. Cruises to Barcelona take place mainly

between April and October. There are a number of routes that combine a visit to the Catalan capital with French and Italian cities such as Nice or Civitavecchia near Rome. A cruise in the Mediterranean Sea is a great way to get to know some of the great southern cities in Europe. The islands of Mallorca and Ibiza, just southeast of Barcelona, are also popular cruise destinations.

5 pp. 174–181 **Miami**

The Miami Design Preservation League (www.mdpl.org) has worked for the preservation, protection and promotion of the Miami Beach Architectural Historic District since 1976. It is the oldest Art Deco association in the world, and has organized annual Art Deco Weekends (usually held in January) since its establishment. The aim is to attract visitors and to promote appreciation of Art Deco style by means of lectures, films, parades, music, shows and other festivities. The association also organizes walks through the Art Deco district guided by local historians and architects.

If you prefer to explore unaccompanied, you can obtain audio information from the Art Deco

Welcome Center seven days a week. Anyone who would like to take in a few Art Deco hotels in Miami Beach can find out more information at www.artdecohotels.com. The website www.miamibeachfl.gov has general information on Miami Beach, as does the expanded site www.miamibeach411.com.

Not for nothing is Miami known as the 'Cruise Capital of the World'. Millions of people set off from here every year, predominantly to the Caribbean or the Bahamas. It is the home port of famous companies such as Carnival Cruise Lines, Norwegian Cruise Line, Royal Caribbean International, Oceania Cruises and Windjammer Barefoot Cruises.

5 pp. 182–191 St Petersburg

The best time for a cruise to St Petersburg is between May and September. Such cruises often also visit Baltic State cities such as Riga (Latvia) and Tallinn (Estonia). Helsinki is another well-known port of call. A number of companies offer cruises that include a visit to St Petersburg. There is also a wide choice of ships.

St Petersburg has a great many sights worth seeing, but a visit to the

Hermitage Museum is an absolute must. To get a foretaste of what the museum has to offer, go to www.hermitagemuseum.org. This fantastic website features a virtual tour of all the rooms in the museum – amazing, but of course it can never beat a real tour, which really requires a minimum of two days. Fortunately a lot of cruise companies stay in port for several days. Information about the city, including tips on day excursions to tourist attractions, can be found at www.petersburg-russia.com or www.saint-petersburg.com. The latter in particular has a wealth of information about the city's history, and there are lots of listings of shops, bars, restaurants and other city 'hot spots'.

A river cruise departing from St Petersburg is an option: a trip to Moscow takes between eight and twelve days. Information about such a journey can be found at www.waytorussia.net and www.visitrussia.com under the heading 'river cruises'. Both sites also have more general information about visas and other practicalities. For detailed and up-to-date information, you can also consult a recognized travel agent.

Practical information
Interesting ports of call

River cruises

6 pp. 198–209 **The Nile**

Several hundred ships cruise down the Nile and there are thousands of cruises along this river each year. Thus there is plenty of choice, and at www.nilecruise.com you can get a first impression of what is possible. The most popular cruise route is between Luxor and Aswan or vice versa, a trip of 220 kilometres (137 miles) that takes four to five days. The cruise ships range from very basic to ultra-luxurious, although it is true that the Egyptian companies can be a little too liberal in their allocation of stars. Nearly all ships have a swimming pool on board and employ English-speaking professionals who accompany passengers on excursions. The longest cruises last twelve days and go from Aswan to Cairo, taking in all the sights on the banks of the longest river in Africa.

In Cairo itself, the Egyptian Museum is highly recommended. There you can see Tutankhamen's death mask, among innumerable other treasures. For more information, go to www.egyptianmuseum.gov.eg. Information about the city is available at www.cairotourist.com. There is a lot of

information about Egypt ancient and modern at www.touregypt.net.

A popular combination is a cruise from Luxor to Aswan, followed by a week's beach holiday on the Red Sea – 'recovery time' after all that spectacular sightseeing.

6 pp. 210–219 **The Rhine**

Cruises on the Rhine are possible the whole year round, including at Christmas, and there are masses to choose from. A good way to begin searching for the right Rhine cruise is to go to www.european-cruise.info/europeanrivercruise/. Here you will find links to a variety of other websites with information about cruises on all the rivers in Europe. Information about the **River Cloud**, which operates regular cruises along the Rhine, can be found at www.seacloud.com. This ship also sails on many other rivers and canals in Germany, Austria, Belgium and the Netherlands.

One of the cities regularly visited as part of a Rhine cruise is Koblenz (www.koblenz.de). Situated where the Rhine meets the Moselle, this city is around 2,000 years old. Cologne is another popular port of call, and you can find lots of references to the museums,

galleries, shops and night life in this beautiful city at www.koeln.de. Similar information for Amsterdam can be found at www.visitamsterdam.nl. Although Amsterdam is not on the Rhine, it is directly connected to it via the Amsterdam–Rhine Canal, and lots of cruises begin and end in this dazzling city. Apart from a trip along the canals, visits to the Rijksmuseum (which has a large collection of Rembrandts) and the Van Gogh Museum are popular day excursions.

6 pp. 220–229 **The Yangtze**

You can also take a cruise along the Yangtze all year round, although there are fewer ships operating between December and March, when the weather is relatively cold. Cruises tend to last between three and nine days. There are some 27 cruise companies operating a total of 60 ships which range from basic to luxurious. The websites www.travelchinaguide.com and www.chinahighlights.com provide information about Yangtze cruises. At www.yangtzecruises.com there is a lot of information about the ships, the river itself and the towns and cities that are visited during a cruise.

One such port of call is the amazingly large city of Chongqing, which is often

the departure or end point of a Yangtze cruise. This industrial metropolis, which is fairly unknown in the West, is home to a staggering 31 million people. For more information go to www. chinats.com. Some 170 kilometres (106 miles) east of this city, on top of the nearly 300-metre (985-foot) high Ming Mountain, lies the tourist attraction of Fengdu, a city of ghosts according to tradition. Here, one can marvel at a number of temples with statues of ghosts and devils. Fortunately these will still be there once construction of the Three Gorges Dam is complete, but the ordinary town will disappear completely under water, to be rebuilt on the other side of the river.

Practical information
River cruises

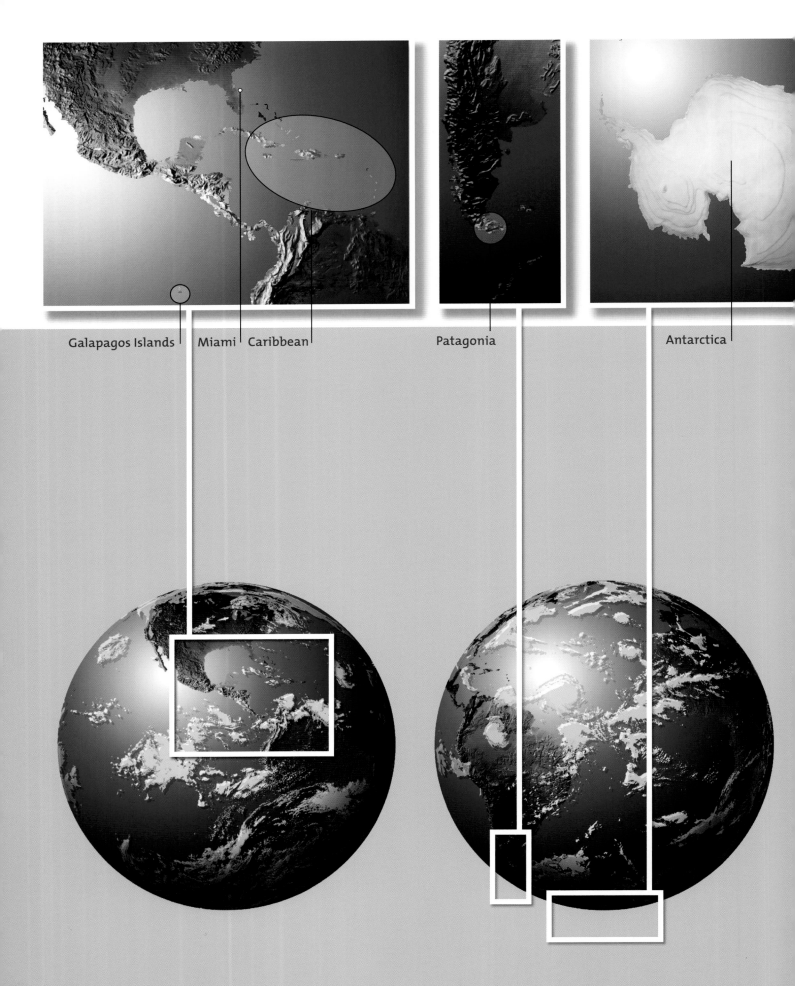

Galapagos Islands | Miami | Caribbean

Patagonia

Antarctica

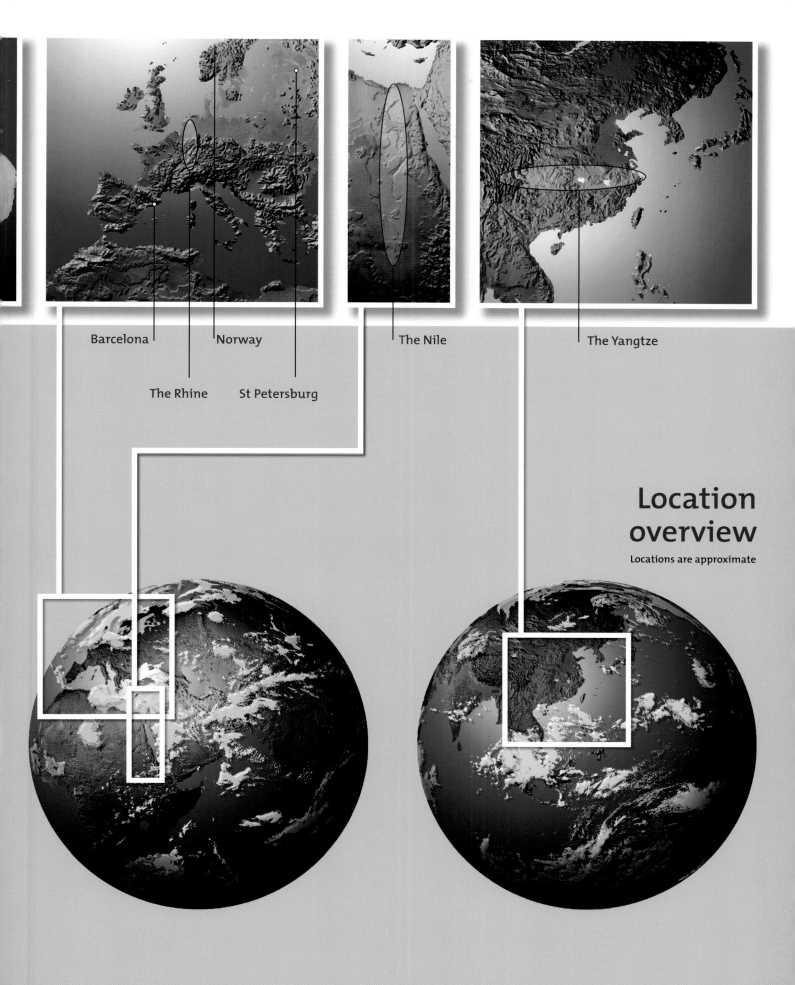

Barcelona

Norway

The Nile

The Yangtze

The Rhine

St Petersburg

Location overview
Locations are approximate

The Caribbean is the absolute number one cruise destination. Around 130 cruise ships carrying predominantly US passengers sail regularly between the region's 7,000 islands and islets. Of course, this does mean ports can become very busy if several mega-ships discharge their passengers all at once. For this reason, a large number of large cruise companies (including Celebrity Cruises, Costa Cruises, Disney Cruises, Holland America Line, Princess Cruises and Royal Caribbean International) have bought or rent their own private islands. Here, guests are greeted on immaculate beaches furnished with all home comforts such as showers, toilets and impromptu bars serving local specialities such as rum punch and banana mamas. Guests can surf, dive and snorkel, bands play 'Island in the Sun', and lifeguards in flowered shirts supervise the swimmers. There is also often a barbecue to round off the perfect Caribbean beach day. Smaller cruise ships often seek out intimate bays to organize similar beach days.

The high season in the Caribbean runs from November (after the hurricane season) until May, and the average length of a cruise is seven days, during which four or more islands are visited, depending on the point of departure.

People setting off from Florida will call at fewer islands than those leaving from Puerto Rico. Cruises in the western Caribbean will have Cozumel, Grand Cayman and Playa del Carmen in their travel schedule. Cruises in the eastern Caribbean will call at islands such as St Thomas (in the US Virgin Islands), Puerto Rico, Martinique and Dominica (not to be confused with the Dominican Republic). Cruises in the southern Caribbean mainly visit islands such as Barbados, Grenada, Aruba and Antigua.

Another destination popular with cruise enthusiasts is the Mediterranean Sea. This body of water is surrounded by many countries, each with its own rich heritage, so a cruise here provides the opportunity to become acquainted with a range of different European and North African cultures. Spain, Italy, Greece and the south of France are high on the list of most European cruisers. City destinations such as Barcelona, Venice, Florence (Livorno) and Athens (Piraeus) also appeal very much to the imagination. The season runs mainly from April to September; less favourable weather conditions mean the Mediterranean is quieter in the winter months, but there are

nonetheless cruises available the whole year round.

Northern Europe is also very popular with cruisers. In actual fact, this is a very old cruise destination: in 1880, Thomas Cooke organized cruises along the coast of Norway from Bergen to above the Arctic Circle. The French writer Paul du Chaillu brought the possibility of such a journey to the attention of the wider public with his book *The Land of the Midnight Sun*. The Norwegian Hurtigruten group has a daily departure from Bergen the whole year round. Nowadays, the Baltic Sea is also a very popular cruise destination, with ports of call such as Helsinki (Finland), Riga (Latvia) and St Petersburg in Russia.

A popular cold cruise destination is the west coast of Alaska. The Glacier Route is typically a one-way cruise between Vancouver and Anchorage or vice versa through the Gulf of Alaska; while the Inside Passage is a circular journey through 1,600 kilometres (1,000 miles) of beautiful inland waterways of Southeast Alaska. As many as sixteen glaciers flow into Glacier Bay National Park, creating a spectacular effect each time a piece of ice breaks off and lands with a crash in the water.

Around Skagway, there is still evidence of the many gold-seekers who once came here to try their luck. Today, this place is experiencing another rush of incomers in the form of the tourists who sweep in on cruise ships. Just imagine: Juneau, with just 3,000 permanent inhabitants and reachable only by ship or aeroplane, is inundated with 750,000 tourists during the brief high season. In order to relieve the pressure on such towns, US cruise companies have created an Alaskan variant of the Caribbean private island: Icy Strait Point is an artificial village of log cabins that has been built specially for tourists at the entrance to Glacier Bay National Park. Here there are numerous shops selling a wide range of souvenirs. The Holland America Line and Princess Cruises have their own hotels, apartments, coaches and even trains in this region.

A cruise through the Panama Canal is also very special. At the moment, most modern cruise ships are too big to make the trip, but with current plans to widen the canal this may change in the next few years. Most cruises through the Panama Canal begin in Florida (Fort Lauderdale) or San Juan (Puerto Rico), and visit a few Caribbean islands before setting off on the nine-hour journey through the canal. The end destination is usually Acapulco, Los Angeles or San Francisco. In the 82 kilometre (51 mile) canal, which runs from northwest to southeast, ships pass through a complex series of locks and lifts that raise them first 26 metres (85 feet) above sea level, and then gradually back down again. At the time of its construction, the Panama Canal was a vast engineering project. It was built by the Americans (having been begun by the French in 1882), and opened in 1914. It cost 387 million dollars, an astronomical sum at the time. Unfortunately, construction also cost around 22,000 lives, mainly because the workers came into contact with contagious diseases. The canal reduced the sailing distance from New York to San Francisco by 12,500 kilometres (7,900 miles); before it was built, ships had to sail around South America, either through the Strait of Magellan or all the way around Cape Horn. This latter option was particularly risky in view of the unpredictable and frequently stormy weather, which claimed numerous shipwrecks over the centuries.

The most popular cruise destinations

Everyone has their own personal preferences when it comes to choosing where to take a cruise. But there remain a few key areas that are the most popular by far among cruisers.

Beaufort scale: a system devised by the English admiral Sir Francis Beaufort in 1805 in which wind force is expressed in figures from 0 to 12. This method was incorporated into international meteorology in 1874. Originally, Beaufort's scale judged the force of the wind by its affect on the sails of a full-rigged ship. Later wind force was allocated a number and a name based on its visible effect on the surface of the sea. Nowadays, therefore, sailors assess the wind force according to the appearance of the sea. The Beaufort scale comprises the following subdivisions:

Wind force 0: Calm. Sea like a mirror. Wind speed is a maximum of 1 knot.

Wind force 1: Light air. Ripples with the appearance of scales are formed, but without foam crests. Wind speed is between 1 and 3 knots.

Wind force 2: Light breeze. Small wavelets, still short but more pronounced; crests have a glassy appearance and do not break. Wind speed is between 4 and 6 knots.

Wind force 3: Gentle breeze. Large wavelets; crests begin to break; foam of glassy appearance; perhaps scattered white horses. Wind speed is between 7 and 10 knots.

Wind force 4: Moderate breeze. Small waves, becoming longer; fairly frequent white horses. Wind speed is between 11 and 16 knots.

Wind force 5: Fresh breeze. Moderate waves, taking a more pronounced long form; many white horses are formed (chance of some spray). Wind speed is between 17 and 21 knots.

Wind force 6: Strong breeze. Large waves begin to form; the white foam crests are more extensive everywhere (probably some spray). Wind speed is between 22 and 27 knots.

Wind force 7: Near gale. Sea heaps up and white foam from breaking waves begins to be blown in streaks along the direction of the wind. Wind speed is between 28 and 33 knots.

Wind force 8: Gale. Moderately high waves of greater length; edges of crests begin to break into spray; the foam is blown in well-marked streaks along the direction of the wind. Wind speed is between 34 and 40 knots.

Wind force 9: Strong gale. High waves; dense streaks of foam along the direction of the wind; crests of waves begin to topple, tumble and roll over; spray may affect visibility. Wind speed is between 41 and 47 knots.

Wind force 10: Storm. Very high waves with long overhanging crests; the resulting foam, in great patches, is blown in dense white streaks along the direction of the wind; on the whole, the surface of the sea takes on a white appearance; the tumbling of the sea becomes heavy and crashing; visibility affected. Wind speed is between 48 and 55 knots.

Wind force 11: Violent storm. Exceptionally high waves (small and medium-sized ships might be for a time lost to view behind the waves); the sea is completely covered with long white patches of foam lying along the direction of the wind; everywhere the edges of the wave crests are blown into froth; visibility affected. Wind speed is between 56 and 63 knots.

Wind force 12: Hurricane. The air is filled with foam and spray; sea completely white with driving spray; visibility very seriously affected. Wind speed is a minimum of 63 knots.

Bow: the foremost part of a ship's hull which ends in the stem.

Bridge: usually an elevated area on a ship from where the captain gives his orders; the command and navigation centre. The bridge is always manned, even when the ship is docked.

Buoy: special sort of (mostly floating) marker to indicate a sailing route on rivers or seas.

Captain: the commander of a ship, the highest position on board.

Captain's cocktail: welcome cocktail, usually served on the second day of a cruise, at which the passengers can meet the captain and his staff. Celebratory event which is usually graced with special cocktails, champagne and hors d'oeuvre offered by the captain.

Captain's dinner: celebratory dinner at the end of a cruise, at which the captain dines together with the passengers. Some passengers have the privilege of being invited by the captain to dine at his table. Normally the captain does not eat in the same room as the passengers during a cruise.

Containership: freight ship specially designed for the transportation of stacked containers.

Crew: personnel who work on a ship.

Cruise director: the person responsible for the entertainment on board a cruise ship.

Drift: sideways movement of a ship under the influence of the wind or a current.

Ferry: usually a large ship designed to carry automobiles and passengers.

Galley: the kitchen on board a ship.

GPS: global positioning system, equipment for determining geographical position by means of satellite reception.

Gross register tonnage (or g.r.t.): see Ship's size.

Harbour pilot: specially trained navigating officer who knows local shallows well and who helps the captain navigate into and out of harbours.

Nautical terms

Hotel Manager: officer in charge of passenger service on a cruise ship.

Hull: main body of a ship, not counting the superstructure, masts and rigging.

Knot: speed in nautical miles per hour.

Leeward side: the side of the ship which is turned away from the wind.

Logbook: see Ship's journal.

Lower deck: deck beneath the main deck of a ship.

Luff: to steer more closely into the wind.

Marine telephone: radio broadcast and receiver apparatus for communication between ships and harbour stations.

Masthead light: white light shining forwards; part of the navigation lighting.

Mayday: necessary cry in ship's radio telephone communication if the ship is in distress (comparable with SOS in ship's radio telegraph communication). 'Mayday' is a corruption of the French 'm'aidez' (help me).

Moor: secure a ship.

Muster station: collection point on a ship where passengers meet in the event of a disaster.

Nautical chart: map of a part of the earth's surface showing the sea and adjacent coastal areas.

Nautical mile: a distance of 1,852 metres (6,080 feet).

Net register tonnage (n.r.t.): see Ship's size.

Ocean liner: large passenger ship designed for travel on the (sometimes rough) ocean at a higher speed than normal cruise ships.

Port: the side of a ship that is on the left when one is facing forward.

Porthole: round window on a ship that is closed by means of clamp bolts.

Purser: the officer responsible for finances. This is often also the person to whom passengers can turn during their stay with questions, requests and complaints about their ship and everything related to their journey.

Radar: apparatus that makes objects and obstacles in and on the water visible on a screen by means of broadcasting high-frequency signals.

Running lights: green light on the starboard side and red light on the port side. These are part of the navigation lighting.

Screw: blade-shaped propeller beneath the waterline used to drive a ship along.

Ship's journal: diary that the captain is obliged to keep or have kept and which contains all the details of a ship's journey (including time spent in port). The description must be such that it can be used to reconstruct the route followed by the ship and any exceptional situations.

Ship's size: expressed in gross register tonnage or g.r.t. A gross register ton is 100 cubic feet (or 2.83 cubic metres). The term 'ton' originally stood for a standard measure of casks in which wine was transported. A ship that could transport five of these casks was therefore five tons in size. The g.r.t. includes all the spaces on a ship that are not open to the sea. The net register ton size

(n.r.t.) is that part of the g.r.t. that is intended for passengers and freight. The n.r.t. is obtained by subtracting from the g.r.t. those compartments housing propulsion engines as well as certain storage areas and crew accommodation.

Ship's symbols:

GTV: Gas Turbine Vessel
MV: Motor Vessel
MS: Motor Sailing yacht
SS: Steamship
SY: Sailing Yacht

Ship's wheel: wheel for steering. In today's computer age, modern cruise ships are steered by means of joysticks.

Stabilizer: equipment that projects from the hull under the water and provides stability when sailing in rough conditions. Stabilizers can be retracted if conditions allow.

Staff captain: second-in-command on board a ship.

Starboard: the side of a ship that is on the right when one is facing forward.

Stateroom: a passenger's private room on board a ship.

Stem: front end (bow) or back end (stern) of a ship.

Stern light: white light shining to the rear, part of the navigation lighting.

Tall ship: sailing vessel, usually two-, three- or four-masted (although the *Royal Clipper* has five).

Tender: a small boat which transports passengers from the ship to the quayside and vice versa if the ship is not able to moor at the quayside.

Tramp ship: cargo vessel not trading regularly between fixed ports, but picking up cargoes wherever obtainable and transporting them to any port.

Windward side: the side of the ship that is turned towards the wind.

Zodiac: sturdy inflatable rubber boat with outboard engine which is used to take passengers to land as part of an excursion. Usually carries between twelve and twenty people.

Nautical terms

United States

Abercrombie & Kent
1520 Kensington Road
Oak Brook, IL 60523-2141. USA
www.aandktours.com

American Canadian Caribbean Line
461 Water Street. P.O. Box 368
Warren, RI 02885. USA
www.accl-smallships.com

American Cruise Lines
One Marine Park
Haddam, CT 06438. USA
www.americancruiselines.com

Blackbeard's Cruises
P.O.Box 661091
Miami , FL 33266. USA
www.blackbeardcruises.com

Carnival Cruise Lines
3655 NW 87 Avenue
Miami, FL 33178–2428. USA
www.carnival.com

Celebrity Cruises
1050 Port Boulevard
Miami, FL 33124. USA
www.celebrity-cruises.com

Clipper Cruise Line
11969 Westline Industrial Drive
St. Louis, Missouri 63146–3220. USA
www.clippercruise.com

Club Med Cruises
75 Valencia Avenue
Coral Gables, FL 33134. USA
www.clubmed.com

Costa Cruises World trade Center
80 SW 8 Street, 27th floor
Miami, FL 33130–3097. USA
www.costacruises.com

Cruise West
2301 Fifth Avenue, Suite 401
Seattle, WA 98121–1856. USA
www.cruisewest.com

Crystal Cruises
2049 Century Park East, Suite 1400
Los Angeles, CA 90067. USA
www.crystalcruises.com

Cunard Line
6100 Blue Lagoon Drive, Suite 400
Miami, FL 33126. USA
www.cunard.com

Discovery World Cruises
1800 S.E 10th Avenue, Suite 205
Fort Lauderdale, FL 33316. USA
www.discoveryworldcruises.com

Disney Cruise Line
Post Office Box 10238
Lake Buena Vista, FL 32830–0238. USA
www.disneycruise.com

Glacier Bay Cruiseline
107 West Denny Way, Suite 303
Seattle, WA 98101. USA
www.glacierbaytours.com

Holland America Line
300 Elliott Avenue West
Seattle, WA 98119. USA
www.hollandamerica.com

Imperial Majesty Cruise Lines
2950 Gateway Drive
Pompano Beach, FL 33069. USA
www.imperialmajesty.com

Lindblad Expeditions
96 Morton Street, 9th floor
New York, NY 10014. USA
www.expeditions.com

MSC Italian Cruises
6750 North Andrews Avenue
Fort Lauderdale, FL 33309. USA
www.msccruisesusa.com

Norwegian Coastal Voyages
405 Park Avenue
New York, NY 10022. USA
www.coastalvoyage.com

Norwegian Cruise Line/ NCL America
7665 Corporate Center Drive
Miami, FL 33126. USA
www.ncl.com

Oceania Cruises
8300 NW 33rd Street, Suite 308
Miami, FL 33122. USA
www.oceaniacruises.com

Orient Lines
7665 Corporate Center Drive
Miami, FL 33126. USA
www.orientlines.com

P&O Cruises 7 Princess Tours
2815 Second Avenue, Suite 400
Seattle Washington 98121–1299. USA
www.pocruises.com

Peter Deilmann Cruises
1800 Diagonal Road, Suite 170
Alexandria, Virginia 22314. USA
www.deilmann-cruises.com

Princess Cruises
24844 Avenue Rockefeller
Santa Clarita, CA 91355. USA
www.princesscruises.com

Quark Expeditions
1019 Boston Post Road
Darien, CT 06820. USA
www.quark-expeditions.com

Radisson Seven Seas Cruises
600 Corporate Drive, Suite 410
Fort Lauderdale, FL 33180. USA
www.rssc.com

ResidenSea Corp.
5200 Blue Lagoon Drive, Suite 790
Miami FL 33126. USA
www.residensea.com

Royal Caribbean International
1050 Caribbean Way
Miami, FL 33132–2096. USA
www.royalcaribbean.com

Sea Cloud Cruises, Inc. U.S. Office
32–40 North Dean Street
Englewood, NJ 07631. USA
www.seacloud.com

Sea Dream Yacht Club
2601 South Bayshore Drive,
Penthouse 1B, Miami, FL 3313. USA
www.seadreamyachtclub.com

Seabourn Cruise Line
6100 Blue Lagoon Drive, Suite 400
Miami, Florida 33126. USA
www.seabourn.com

Silversea Cruises
110 East Broward Boulevard
Fort Lauderdale, FL 33301. USA
www.silversea.com

Cruise company addresses

Most of the big cruise companies are based in the United States. Companies move frequently, so it is wise to check these addresses on the internet.

United States (continued)

Star Clippers
7200 NW 19th Street, Suite 206
Miami, FL 33126. USA
www.star-clippers.com

Swan Hellenic Kartagener
631 Commack Road, Suite 1A
Commack, NY 11725. USA
www.swanhellenic.com

Travel Dynamics International
132 East 70th Street
New York, NY 10021. USA
www.traveldynamicsinternational.com

Windjammer Barefoot Cruises
1759 Bay Road, P.O. Box 190120 Miami
Beach, FL 33119–0120. USA
www.windjammer.com

Windstar Cruises
300 Elliott Avenue West
Seattle, WA 98119. USA
www.windstarcruises.com

Yangtze Cruises Inc.
566 7th Ave, Suite 506
New York, NY 10018. USA
www.yangtzecruises.com

Elsewhere

Aida Cruises
Am Seehafen 1, Siemenstrasse 90
63203 New Isenberg, Germany
www.aida.de

Antarctic Shipping S.A.
Av. Vitacura 2771, of. 904
Santiago, Chile
www.antarctic.cl

Blue Lagoon Cruises
P.O. Box 130
Lautoka, Fiji Islands
www.bluelagooncruises.com

Costa Crociere (Costa Cruises)
Via Gabriele d'Annunzio 2/80
16121 Genoa, Italy
www.costacruises.com

Delphin Seereisen GmbH
Neusalzer Straße 22e
63069 Offenbach, Germany
www.delphin-cruises.com

Discovery Cruises UK Ltd
15 Young Street, Kensington
London W8 5EH, UK
www.discoveryworldcruises.com

Fred Olsen Cruise Lines
Fred Olson House, White House Road,
Ipswich, Suffolk 1P1 5LL, UK
www.fredolsen.co.uk

Golden Star Cruises
85 Akti Miaouli
Piraeus, Greece 185 38
www.goldenstarcruises.com

Hansa Touristik
Contrescarpe 36
D-28203 Bremen, Germany
www.hansatouristik.de

Hapag-Lloyd Kreitzfahrten GmbH
Ballindamm 25
D-20095 Hamburg, Germany
www.hlkf.com

Hebridean Island Cruises
Kintail House, Carleton New Road,
Skipton, North Yorkshire, BD23 2DE, UK
www.hebridean.co.uk

Hurtigruten Group ASA
Havnegata 2, Postboks 43
8514 Narvik, Norway
www.hurtigruten.com

Island Cruises
Island House, Kestrel Court, 213–215
Broadway, Salford, M50 2UE, UK
www.islandcruises.com

Kristina Cruises
Kirkkokatu 16
48100 Kotka, Finland
www.kristinacruises.com

Louis Cruise Lines
274 Main Road, Sutton-at-Hone,
Dartford, Kent, UK
www.louiscruises.com

Mitsui OSK Passenger Line
Shuwa-Kioicho Park Building, Kioicho
3–6, Chiyoda-ku, Tokyo 192-8552, Japan
www.mopas.co.jp.com

MSC Cruises
Via A. Depretis 31, 80133 Naples, Italy
www.msccruises.com

Nippon Yusen Kaisha (NYK) Line
Yusen Building, 3–2 Marunouchi 2-
choime, Chiyoda-ku 100-0005, Japan
www.asukacruise.co.jp

Ocean Village Holidays
Richmond House, Terminus Terrace
Southampton SO14 3PN, UK
www.oceanvillageholidays.co.uk

Orient Lines
1 Derry Street, Kensington,
London W8 5NN, UK
www.orientlines.com

P&O Cruises
Richmond House, Terminus Terrace
Southampton SO14 3PN, UK
www.pocruises.com

P&O Cruises Australia
P.O. Box 5387, Sydney 2001
New South Wales, Australia
www.pocruises.com.au

Phoenix Seereisen
Kolmstrasse 50, 53111 Bonn, Germany
www.phoenixreisen.com

Ponant Cruises
60 Boulevard Marchal Juin
44100 Nantes, France
www.ponant.com

Radisson Seven Seas Cruises UK Ltd
Suite 3 & 4 Canute Chambers
Canute Road, Southampton
SO15 3AB, UK
www.shipsandcruises.com

Saga Holidays & Cruises Ltd
Freepost, Folkestone
Kent CT20 3SE, UK
www.sagacruises.com

Silversea Cruises
77/79 Great Eastern Street
London EC2A 3HU, UK
www.silversea.com

Sea Cloud Cruises
Ballindamm 17
D-200095 Hamburg, Germany
www.seacloud.com

Star Clippers
Ermenno Palace 27, Boulevard Albert 1er
98000 Monaco
www.star-clippers.com

Star Cruises
1 Shenton Way 01–02, Singapore 068803
www.starcruises.com

Swan Hellenic Cruises
Richmond House, Terminus Terrace
Southampton SO14 3PN, UK
www.swanhellenic.com

Thomson Cruises
Wigmore House, Wigmore Place,
Wigmore Lane, Luton LU2 9TN, UK
www.thomson-holidays.com

Transocean Tours
Stavendamm 22, D-28195 Bremen,
Germany
www.transocean.de

Venus Cruise
Umeda Hanshin Daiichi Building
5–25 Umeda 2 chome
Kita-ku, Osaka 530-0001, Japan
www.venus-cruise.co.jp

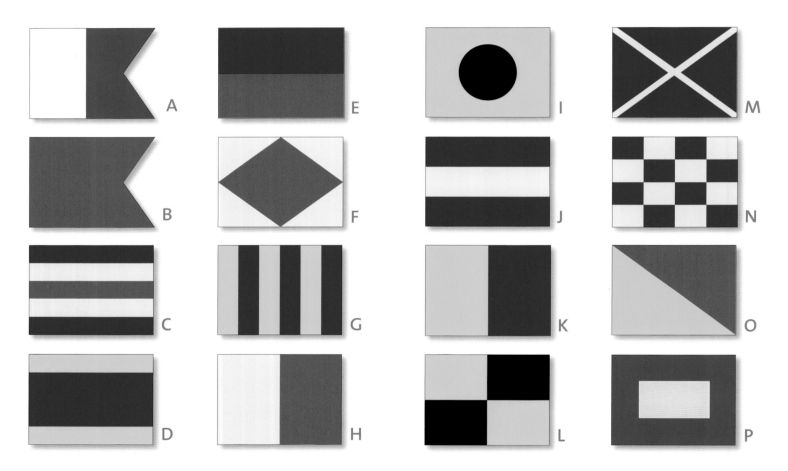

There are 40 code flags in all, 26 alphabetical, 10 numerical pennants, 3 substitutes and the code pennant. Signals are made in one-, two-, three-, and four-letter flag hoists.

Single-letter signals are both for emergencies and everyday use:

A (Alfa): I have a diver down; keep well clear at slow speed.

B (Bravo): I am taking in, or discharging, or carrying dangerous goods.

C (Charlie): Yes.

D (Delta): Keep clear of me; I am manoeuvring with difficulty.

E (Echo): I am altering my course to starboard.

F (Foxtrot); I am disabled; communicate with me.

G (Golf): I require a pilot.

H (Hotel): I have a pilot on board.

I (India): I am altering my course to port.

J (Juliet): I am on fire and have dangerous cargo on board; keep well clear of me.

K (Kilo): I wish to communicate with you.

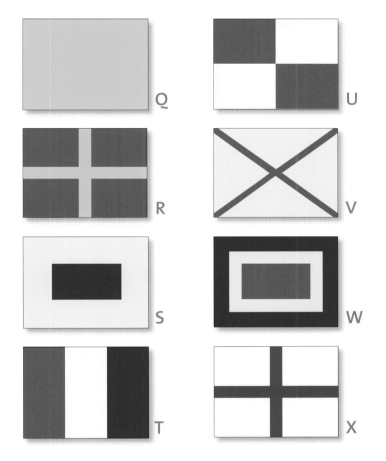

Signal flags

Signal flags are internationally used in the nautical world. In times past they were the only way ships could communicate with each other. Radio communication may have taken over, but flags still come in handy: for instance, when a ship in harbour raises the P-flag (the Blue Peter), any crew ashore know to report on board immediately as it is about to set out to sea.

L (Lima): You should stop your vessel instantly.

M (Mike): My vessel is stopped and making no way through the water.

N (November): No (negative).

O (Oscar): Man overboard.

P (Papa): In harbour: all persons should report on board.
At sea (fishing vessel): my nets have got caught on an obstruction.

Q (Quebec): My vessel is healthy and I request free pratique (licence to enter port).

R (Romeo): I have received your signal.

S (Sierra): My engines are going astern.

T (Tango): Keep clear of me; I am engaged in pair trawling.

U (Uniform): You are running into danger.

V (Victor): I require assistance.

W (Whiskey): I require medical assistance.

X (X-ray): Stop carrying out your intentions and watch for my signals.

Y (Yankee): I am dragging my anchor.

Z (Zulu): I require a tug.

Index